A HOLISTIC GUIDE TO EMBRACING PREGNANCY, CHILDBIRTH, AND MOTHERHOOD

A HOLISTIC GUIDE TO EMBRACING PREGNANCY, CHILDBIRTH, AND MOTHERHOOD

❀ ❀ ❀

Wisdom and Advice from a Doula

BY KAREN SALT

PERSEUS
PUBLISHING

A Member of the Perseus Books Group

Cataloging-in-Publication Data available from the Library of Congress.
ISBN 1-55561-282-2

Perseus Publishing is a Member of the Perseus Books Group.

Find us on the World Wide Web at http://www.perseuspublishing.com

Perseus Publishing books are available at special discounts for bulk purchases in the U.S. by corporations, institutions, and other organizations. For more information, please contact the Special Markets Department at the Perseus Books Group, 11 Cambridge Center, Cambridge, MA 02142, or call (800) 255-1514 or (617) 252-5298, or e-mail j.mccrary@perseusbooks.com.

Text design by Reginald Thompson
Set in 11-point New Caledonia by the Perseus Books Group

First printing, December 2002
1 2 3 4 5 6 7 8 9 10—06 05 04 03 02

TABLE OF CONTENTS

ACKNOWLEDGMENTS

To Jessica Porter for giving me a push so many years ago

To Debra Pascali-Bonaro for seeing in me a kindred spirit

To Sarah Trotta for being a talented editor and a brilliant friend

To Marnie Cochran, Lolly Axley, and the immensely creative professionals at Perseus Publishing for offering me guidance and support

To David, Liam, Seamus, and Moira for being such a gifted family: You bring out the best in me.

And finally to the millions of women who will give birth this year: May you embrace the magic and the mystery of mothering.

INTRODUCTION

A pregnant mother today has a myriad of sources available to her on childbirth and baby care. Classes, books, Web pages, and professionals provide hours of information on various topics, but rarely from a holistic perspective.

"Holistic" is an ancient word that is enjoying renewal thanks to society's interest in natural living. In its simplest form, holism refers to a life approach of placing the parts of something into a balanced whole. From a health standpoint, holistic becomes even more, concerning itself with the interconnectedness of the mind, body, and spirit, as well as the need to respond and enrich each part of a whole person in order for him or her to achieve wellness.

Material that concentrates on only one aspect of your mind, body, or spirit ignores the powerful forces that affect the others. This is one reason why I wrote this book. My interest in living holistically isn't a new trend or a sudden occurrence. Socrates philosophized about it in ancient Greece. In India, a system of healing called Ayurveda, or the science of life or longevity, originated more than five thousand years ago.

But holism isn't just something historical; it is also something that women and men today, forced to live faster, take less time to enjoy existing, and manage greater stressors, want to achieve. Best-selling authors Deepak Chopra and Andrew Weil continue to respond to the overwhelming desire that people have to live healthily, exist in harmony with their environment, and find balance in a world that is, at times, turbulent.

As a whole person, you deserve holistic material that recognizes that you are more than a pregnant person about to give birth. You are a friend, a lover, a daughter, and a woman. You are all of these things and more as you navigate pregnancy, experience birth, and travel through motherhood.

A Holistic Guide to Embracing Pregnancy, Childbirth, and Motherhood: Wisdom and Advice from a Doula grows out of this interest and presents you, a mother in the making, with information that shows you the strength you have within yourself to birth your baby with joy, love, and confidence. Yet this book covers more than just childbirth. It outlines pregnancy information and postpartum concerns that affect a mother's mind, body, and spirit. These are details often neglected in pregnancy and birth books: Staying connected with a partner, finding joy in the little things in life, eating naturally healthy foods, reducing stress, filling life with positive energy, birthing with confidence, resuming intimacy with a lover after birth, and simply mothering from the heart.

I have written this book out of my experience as a doula. Doulas are advocates of mothers and their families who offer continuous support and information during pregnancy, birth, and the early period of postpartum.

Doulas are not cookie-cutter replicas of one another. Each has her own unique style and presentation. Within these pages you will find mine. It is a brief offering of the positive energy, support, and information that doulas give mothers. I offer it as I do myself: with humble respect for mothers like you.

Part One

❈ ❈ ❈

EMBRACING PREGNANCY

Pregnancy is defined in many medical dictionaries as being with child. This simple description does not convey the magic, the pleasure, or the surreal craziness of growing a new life.

Women who get to this place in their lives have chosen, risked, or even accidentally found themselves in this position. Regardless of circumstance, being pregnant is a blessing and perhaps a challenge for the newly pregnant woman who is stretched, for the first time, to accommodate so many changes in her mind, body, and spirit.

Many pregnant mothers' thoughts drift often to their due dates. Their baby's birth consumes so much of their mental, physical, and spiritual energy that they spend most of their pregnancy thinking about birth and getting ready for it.

You too are probably consumed by thoughts of your baby's birth. This absorption is normal. You should be spending time and energy considering how and with whom your baby will enter the world.

But pregnancy is more than the months between conception and birth. It is a crucial time that helps a mother go from pondering motherhood to experiencing it.

Throughout Part 1, I redefine concepts and explore new ideas about pregnancy in order for you to seize your procreative power as a mother. As a doula, I believe that mothers are beautiful. It is my sincerest wish for you to embrace that idea as well.

Part 1 consists of three chapters that holistically explore pregnancy by examining how it affects your mind, body, and spirit. It is possible to experience pregnancy in the same intensely sensory way you hope to experience your baby's birth. Embrace this time and revel in it.

1

❋ ❋ ❋

YOUR PREGNANT MIND

Pregnancy is a time of adjustments. Just when you think you have things under control, another change throws you off track. Stretch marks appear in skin that was smooth just yesterday. Bathroom visits challenge a full night's sleep. And to top it off, you feel emotional about everything. Commercials make you cry. Baby clothes make you misty. People you love can suddenly make you angry. Your emotions are in a frenzy, soaring from one extreme to the next as you struggle to navigate the many forces in your mind.

Compounding this, of course, is your concern and apprehension about your baby's growth and development. Sometimes it feels like there are too many things to think about: the sex of your baby, breast-feeding, strollers, and even premature thoughts about your baby's college fund can fight for space in your already crowded mind. It can feel like everything is moving in a circle around you in a never-ending spiral of things to consider.

At moments like this, it's good to call a time-out and break the cycle of anxiety. You are the one person who can decide what kind of pregnancy you will have. Why? Because you are the one experiencing it.

It is a part of you and exists within you—especially your mind. Many mothers are pregnant but not within their thoughts. Their thoughts fluctuate from being "taken over" by something they have no control over to "embarking" on a journey that they suspect they are not qualified for.

You too may be playing the mental game of uncertainty as you strive to become the mother that you are meant to be. To embrace your pregnancy fully, you have to allow this experience to fill your mind, positively, with the beauty and the blessings of this journey. Start today by helping your mind connect you to the baby you are creating.

If you allow anxiety and stress to crowd your mind, you can give yourself more than just a few unpleasant thoughts.

Your body has a built-in reaction to situations or events that are anxiety inducing or relaxing. This reaction eventually signals the body's autonomic nervous system, a river system of nerves that has two parts. On one side is the magical part that stimulates the body to make hormones that promote feelings of tranquillity and relaxation. You can sense this when you soak your aching feet at the end of a long day or receive a gentle neck massage. The oohs and aahs that express your sense of warmth and serenity are simply a response to the pleasurable hormones coursing through your body.

But those hormones are not the ones you will encounter when the second part of the autonomic nervous system functions. This part pours out the nerve triggers that stimulate the fight-or-flight response that adds adrenaline to the bloodstream just in case action is needed. For a pregnant mom, this means less blood flow to her uterus—and her baby—and more blood flow to her arms and legs. This stress affects the baby by increasing his heartbeat and flooding his tiny body with stress hormones. A mother's body can suffer muscle cramps, increased heart rate, and other problems if the body stays in a prolonged state of heightened stress.

All in all, stress, anxiety, and tension are not good for a mom or her baby. How then do you remove them from your life?

Adopt a simple strategy of reducing the challenges, concerns, and uncertainties in life. Studies show that participating regularly in the types of relaxing tips mentioned in this chapter can lower a mother's blood pressure, lower her stress level, increase her agility, and enhance her connection with her baby.

Here are four easy-to-follow relaxation techniques.

RELAXATION IDEA 1

The first thing that I want you to do is easy: Slow down to experience life—smell a few flowers, marvel at the sunset, and acknowledge the growing life inside you. When you walk to the nearest store, stroll. When you are on the subway, take a few quiet minutes to reflect on your baby versus planning last-minute details for the day ahead. Simply slow things down so that you can "hear" life. There are no hard-and-fast rules for experiencing moments with your baby or appreciating all of the good things around you.

Once you are in the habit of focusing your energy and attention on your baby and yourself, relaxing becomes easier.

CONNECTION

As a mother, you are connected to things on a deeper, more intimate level: the things you have placed in certain parts of your home, the friends and coworkers who interact with you, and the mothers who have come before you and the ones who have yet to be.

Throughout your life, connections to many things will be made and broken, sustained and stabilized. During this pregnancy, pay attention to the connections that are in and around you.

Relaxation can involve more than just the occasional good thought or stroll among the flowers. It can encompass touch, massage, meditation, and other techniques utilized to remove distractions from your life and focus your energy on basic things like breathing. This type of focus is often used during labor, but it has an equally important role during pregnancy. It can bring your baby into your life as more than just an abstract thought.

RELAXATION IDEA 2: CONNECTING WITH YOUR BABY

Read the exercise in its entirety first, so that you have some idea what it involves. Then try doing it.

1. Sit in a comfortable place—perhaps against the headboard of your bed or in a roomy chair. Turn off the ringer of the telephone. Surround yourself with pillows if that will help you relax.
2. Once seated, slow down your breathing. Place your hands on either side of your lower back, just above the top of your hips. Take in a deep breath that expands the muscles under your hands.
3. Breathe deeply but watch for feelings of dizziness or discomfort. If you feel fine, continue. Focus on the basic rhythms of your heartbeat or the air around you. Feel your body strengthen. Notice how your thoughts sink deep inside your mind. Discover how the place where you are seated almost seems to take your body and tenderly cradle it. This may take minutes or tens of minutes to happen. The length of time needed depends on your willingness to experience quiet. As you continue to practice this exercise, reaching this quiet place will eventually take less and less time.
4. Now focus your thoughts further into yourself to the place where your baby is growing. Close your eyes.

Visualize, in your mind, your breath entering your body and traveling like a cloud of energy into your lungs, into your blood, into your baby. Visualize your baby responding to this energy. He or she may even wiggle or turn inside your uterus in response to your breath. Feel your breath spread through the umbilical cord, coating your baby in your life force.

5. As you exhale, notice the air that is leaving your body. Envision stress and uncertainty leaving your body as you blow out. Listen to and notice the way the air moves in and out. Tell yourself that any apprehension and tension that you are holding is being released with each exhalation. Try not to force your breath to move faster in order to release more tension. Your breathing should be smooth and unhurried. Breathe in and out slowly. Devote as much time as you need to this activity.

6. Once you are ready to end the exercise, slowly open your eyes. Adjust your vision and your senses. Journey from inside your body to the environment outside your body. Look at your room. Look at the world around you. Notice the freshness of the air. Increase your breathing until it returns to a normal pace.

7. When you feel comfortable resuming activity, stretch, turn the ringer of the telephone back on, and continue with your day.

8. End of exercise.

Visualization is powerful. Did you notice how your breath moved through your body, something you do unconsciously every moment of every day? Did your visualize your baby? What did he or she look like in your mind?

There are moms who have a clear image of their little ones in their mind's eye. These moms tend to have detailed dreams about their babies on a daily basis.

Other moms have a hard time visualizing their babies before they are born, almost as if they are pregnant with "something" that they cannot imagine will come out as a baby. Both of these are normal reactions and may be experienced during the same week. So how do you sustain the connection with your baby even if she is an abstract image in your mind? Keep a journal.

I keep a journal in my private life and in my professional one. My private one records my crazy thoughts and burgeoning feelings about every facet of my life. My professional one records similar things. It is the place where I shed my confusion, concern, and admiration about maternity care in America. This sacred place allows me, as a doula, to get rid of feelings about the health care system that have no place in my relationship with a mother and her family. When I excise them, good or bad, my thoughts become organized, allowing my mission to remain clear.

Your journal can be something as simple as a spiral-bound notebook or something as elaborate as a detailed book that includes clippings and photographs. Thanks to a resurgent interest in journaling, you can find beautiful journals for pregnant moms at your nearest bookstore. Many have been arranged with specific exercises that can help you connect and understand the many changes that you are going through. Some mothers give pregnancy journals as keepsakes to their babies after birth. This is a kind of record of the highlights of the pregnancy that they hope to share with their babies.

Journaling can also be a private thing. You can share your thoughts on becoming a mother and your concerns about many segments of your life—including your relationship with your partner. This critically important person can be just as consumed by the changes of pregnancy as you are. The difference is that he cannot experience what you are feeling. The solution is not to ignore him or tell him that he does not understand. Instead, communicate to him how you are adjusting and developing into a mother, and listen to his thoughts about becoming a father. You are both affected by this journey, no matter how obvious your changes may be compared to his.

This pregnancy is your experience alone, but, hopefully, it is one that you can share. From supporting your nutrition needs to massaging your hard-working body, your partner can play a part in helping you connect your pregnancy with your mind (and his), allowing both of you to relax and enjoy this time.

One great way to connect and relax with your partner is through simple, nonsexual touch. I bet you never thought someone could touch you and bring you a sense of relaxation, but it is true. At the core of touch is the awareness that two people can unite, for even a brief moment, and share their energy with each other. Doulas utilize touch, when appropriate and permitted, to convey strength, courage, respect, and admiration to a woman as she undertakes the role of a lifetime: motherhood.

Touch, though, can also unite a person's mind, body, and spirit, helping balance and alignment to occur. During stressful or fearful moments, this energy transfer can be healing. I'm not the only one who believes this. Universities are waking up to the benefits of touch therapy with patients by offering it as a course for medical and nursing students. The power of touch for healing has received major research and news coverage. According to the Web site of Healing Touch International, more than thirty thousand nurses in hospitals across the United States use hands-on touch each year. Touch has also become an international movement. Universities in Paris, the Philippines, California, and Miami all have Touch Research Institutes that further chronicle the medical benefits of touch therapy.

But touch is not just limited to healing purposes. It can also be used to transfer strength and energy to someone. Has your partner ever held your hand when you were nervous or scared because you asked him to or because he wanted you to know that things were going to be okay? If you said yes, then you know the power of touch therapy. If your partner has never given you that sort of touch, filter through your memories in your mind and insert the person who has. That person has probably offered you a shoulder, a hug, or a hand when you needed it. This type of appropriate, nonsexual touching is touch therapy.

Perhaps one of the biggest rumors about touch therapy is that someone has to be trained to use it effectively. That's not true. Anyone can give comfort to someone else through touch. Doulas touch when appropriate with moms as a way to say, "I am here for you." This is a message that your partner may want to give you as well.

Here is a touch exercise that I often encourage moms to do with their partners in my childbirth classes. I want you and your partner to try it.

RELAXATION IDEA 3:
CONNECTING WITH YOUR PARTNER

Read the exercise once so that you are aware of what it entails and then give it a try.

1. Sit comfortably against the headboard of your bed or rest against a large pile of pillows in a chair. Ask your partner to join you. He should be sitting comfortably facing you. Close your eyes. If you are comfortable, remove your clothes to encourage a more intimate touch.
2. Turn off the lights, the television, and the phone. Let silence fill both of you as you become aware of nothing except each other.
3. When aware of the breath of your partner flowing around you, ask your partner to gently skim both of his hands over your body from your head to your toes. If you have chosen to keep your clothes on, he can touch you over your clothing. If you are naked, his fingers should lightly brush your skin. The touch

that he is doing is called effleurage. It is a light, almost fluttery touch that can feel good. It is not supposed to be deep, muscular tissue contact.

4. While he is touching your body, do not speak to each other. Together, simply breathe in and out. Let your shared breath fill your soul and rejuvenate you.

5. Continue the massage for as long as needed—until the touch brings about the relaxed state sought.

6. After a time, your partner should check your body for areas that are still tense. Have him make a gentle sweep of your skin with his hands. This last pass over your skin should draw the last lingering strands of tension away.

7. End of exercise. *Note:* In many ways, this kind of touching is an intense, intimate moment with the person offering the effleurage. If you feel uncomfortable doing this sort of exercise with your partner, please choose someone else you trust to participate with you.

Now that you have completed the exercise, how do you feel? Were you aware of your partner beside you during the exercise? What did his touch feel like? Was it comfortable?

Some moms love this type of light stroke. Others need a more intense massage in order to release tension and feel a deeper connection with others. For a professional massage, contact the National Association of Pregnancy Massage Therapy. They can provide you with contact names of massage therapists who are trained and certified in maternity massage. Receiving a massage during pregnancy can be just what you need to release tension, calm your thoughts, and rejuvenate your mind.

PROFESSIONAL MASSAGE
Professionals trained in the specifics of a pregnant mother's body are the only people who should perform deep tissue,

therapeutic body massage. Some doulas offer massage as a service to mothers. Before agreeing to this service, ask about her training and background. Always choose someone who is a CMT—certified massage therapist.

The cost of a prenatal or maternity massage is between $40 and $75. An additional cost of $10–$20 can get you your own massage therapist in your home for a short period of time. Sessions usually last about an hour. Contact the National Association of Pregnancy Massage Therapy at 888-457-4945, or on the Internet at: napmt.home.texas.net for more information.

Sometimes, a simple gesture can achieve the same results as a massage. A hand gently placed on the shoulder may give you all the comfort you need. This is something that your partner may offer you every day.

Feel his touch and touch him in return. Encourage him to touch the life that you have created together. You can achieve this kind of shared connection by doing the following exercise I call a "baby cuddle."

RELAXATION IDEA 4: BABY CUDDLING

A baby cuddle is similar to a chest-to-back hug.

1. Sit with your legs comfortably in front of you while your partner nestles behind you.
2. With your back against his chest, have your partner surround you with his arms and rest his hands on your round belly.
3. Place your hands on top of his and cuddle your baby together.
4. Lightly stroke your skin, drawing the shape of your baby within your womb.

5. Continue as long as this feels comfortable.
6. End of exercise.

TOUCHING YOUR SKIN WITH OIL

Purchase some massage oil from a store that specializes in bath and body products. Because your skin is stretched and sensitive, be sure to select a product that does not smell offensive to you or dry out your skin. Next, choose a comfortable spot somewhere in your home. Once you are comfortable, lift up or take off your shirt to expose your belly. Pour a little oil into the palm of your hand to warm it up. Rub your hands together to help spread it around. When you are ready, place a hand on each side of your belly. Move each hand in a sideways figure eight formation. Take your time with this. Enjoy the feeling of oil on your skin. Talk to your baby if you want to. Imagine that your baby can feel each gentle movement. Note the response to your touch. Recognize that your hands are cradling your baby as your body has cradled her all these months. Say hello to your little one.

Cuddling with your baby and touching your partner are just a few of the ways you can help your mind achieve a calmer and more relaxed state.

LIGHT, SCENTS, MUSIC, AND WATER

Using one of the five senses to soothe the mind is often a form of "meditation by association." You may associate the scent of lavender with a lavender-scented pillow you snuggled against on your grandmother's couch as a child. Similarly, the feel of warm water may remind you of the warm watering holes that you found in your youth. Each memory elicits remembrances from you. These are memories you can connect with and bring back into your life.

Here is a list of sensory-rich ideas that can erase tension from your mind and replace it with more pleasant thoughts and feelings. Choose the type of comfort that will bring you relaxation. If you do not know which one might work best, try them all!

Light. Candles and other lights pull in your visual sense. Watching a candle burn is an act of gazing at life; the flame responds to wind, oxygen, and energy as if it were alive. Start a light ritual just for yourself. Set up a special, safe place in your home where you can light a candle and refresh your mind. Even the smallest corner of a house can become your own important location. Although any place will work, you need to choose a place that is not crowded with people.

Use as many candles as you wish. The goal is to release tension, breathe deeply, and acknowledge your pregnancy, your baby, and yourself.

Some moms find that this type of ritual helps them greet each day with renewed mental strength and energy. You may find that you cannot make a daily commitment. If you would like to bring this ritual into your life, bring it in on your time, fitting it into your schedule as you see fit.

You can also enjoy the power of light without resorting to burning candles. One way is to turn down your bright, fluorescent lights at work or at home, leaving only the shallow glow of sidelights—or perhaps no lights at all. Certain types of lighting can affect relaxation and even tension in the body. Extremely bright or harsh overhead lights can promote headaches and fatigue.

Our world is populated with an abundance of lights. Unless you live outside a metro area, you encounter streetlights, porch lights, business lights, and other shining examples of humanity every day. While this lighting can illuminate the darkness, it can also pull one away from the beauty of the natural world.

Enjoy the natural light of the world by watching a sunset or sitting quietly in a darkened room listening to a symphony of natural sound.

Scents.   Smells can relax the chaos of the mind. If you know that certain scents relax you, look for candles or other aromatic sources that can add these relaxing aromas into your home. Bubble baths, potpourri, and incense are options. A word of warning: Not every smell is wonderful once you take it from the store and use it in your home. Some items only give off an aroma in their packaging. Once the scent diffuses in the air, nothing remains. Other items have an overpowering odor that dominates everything. To make the best choice, purchase items in small quantities and test them first. If you are buying bath oil, buy the smallest bottle possible. Purchase potpourri in small ounces and check for recommended use. Some potpourris require heating in oil or water. Always check a product for ease of use and ingredients.

Massage oils are another wonderful scented choice. Choices abound for flavors and combinations. I usually test the scented massage oils that I use with a mom. I ask her what scent she enjoys and then bring that oil with me to a prenatal visit where I can test it on her arm. Many times a loved scent is abandoned when it irritates the skin or smells unpleasant.

Music.   Music relaxes us in subtle ways. Sometimes lyrics soothe us or charge our souls. Other times, it's the rhythm or the searing guitar riffs that lighten our hearts. From John Lee Hooker to Frank Sinatra, we all have our favorite music that can help us relax or let go of tension.

When you find songs that you enjoy, use the latest technology to create your own compilation CDs or tapes of the music. I collect what I call "mood tapes" that I can play when I am traveling in my car or writing. Writing a relaxing passage is easier when I am listening to relaxing music. The same rings true for uplifting information.

You can use music to enhance or release certain mental energy. Let the music encourage your body to move, stretch, and dance. If you choose to dance, try not to overtax yourself. Simple hip movements from side to side can be enough. Dancing, even lightly swaying, is such a stress reliever that you might find yourself dancing with your partner now and during labor.

Water. There is something elemental about water. Maybe it is because our bodies are made up of about 90 percent water that we enjoy it surrounding us. Many women feel at home in it.

There are a number of ways to add water to your life to enrich you mentally. One easy way is to swim. Swimming is gentle on the expanding body and joints of a pregnant mother. It also provides a mild workout that does not jar the bones or stress the body.

If you are unable to swim because of health or practical reasons, you can take warm baths or showers.

Try this: Fill your tub with warm water. Be careful. Water that is too hot can harm your baby. Place enough water in the tub to cover your belly.

Before you get in, place a cold glass of water or fruit juice for yourself on the side of the tub or a nearby counter just in case you become thirsty. You can also increase your relaxation within the water by adding your favorite bath oil or arranging candles on the counter around the sink.

Next, climb in safely. Use the handrails or a supportive arm from your partner if you feel unsteady.

Once in the water, think about nothing. Empty your mind. Dinner does not exist. Meetings do not exist. Only that moment in time exists. Rub your belly if you want. Rest comfortably as long as you can.

Your mind, the amazing organ that drives so much of your consciousness, benefits greatly from relaxing and visualizing. It is the center of much thought and stress about various issues. Ironically, it is also the part of a pregnant woman that she may ignore as she focuses her energy on being pregnant.

The holistic focus of this book starts with a central part of the your body, your mind, but does not ignore your body, the part of you that "is" pregnant and is immensely affected by this journey.

Now that you are mentally fortified, let's move on to examining how pregnancy affects your body.

2

❋ ❋ ❋

YOUR PREGNANT BODY

Your body is the temple that holds, nurtures, and sustains your baby throughout this pregnancy. While it openly announces your state of motherhood to any and all who gaze at it, your body does an amazing amount of work quietly growing your baby from a single cell into the thriving, squirming bundle that will soon be nestled in your arms. It draws on ancestral, inherent biological knowledge to bring your baby into the world.

Living a life of balance and strength allows one to experience pregnancy as a time of healing as well as growth. For the body to live in balance, it must be given a healthy foundation. The benefits are enormous and reach beyond pregnancy. Research studies show that healthier mothers have shorter labors and recover faster after birth. These results say it all: Living healthy results in being healthy. But how do you achieve a healthier lifestyle? By concentrating on nutritious eating and smart lifestyle choices.

NUTRITIOUS EATING

A pregnant woman's body changes dramatically throughout her pregnancy as every single cell works to grow and sustain her baby. Her breasts count for about three pounds. Her uterus increases to about two and one-half pounds. Extra blood and fluid circulate throughout her system. Every part of her body is geared to assist the development of her baby and her body to care for him.

WEIGHT GAIN DURING PREGNANCY
Women gain weight at different times throughout their pregnancies. You may gain more pounds one month than you do the next. In most cases, this is not worrisome. Your doctor or midwife will monitor your weight gain. This is not because you should only gain a certain amount of weight during your pregnancy. They check weight gain because some medical concerns or problems during pregnancy first appear as too much or too little weight gain.

This fact is often lost in the nutrition information contained in most pregnancy material and in the advice shared by friends. Most of it focuses on what a mother should and should not eat, mostly to avoid gaining unnecessary weight. It does not view nutrition from the standpoint of what is needed to grow a healthy baby and sustain a healthy baby.

There are many subtle messages in our society that imply pregnant women resemble "beached whales." These negative ideas can distort a mother's perception of her physical self.

Amazingly, a pregnant mother walking with full breasts and a distended belly full of a vital child is characterized in our society as waddling like a duck—language mothers themselves sometimes use. This image is in complete opposition to the powerful concept of mothers as sustainers of life, as the only humans capable of birthing babies.

To find your power, shift your concept of your body. Acknowledge the changes taking place but concentrate on the beauty and the blessings of the adaptations. Yes, you are changing, but that is because your baby needs you to become this new person in order to keep him alive.

When you consider how important your role is in your baby's development, it makes sense to keep your body in optimum health. To do that, think about what you eat.

Take a moment right now to list every food item that you ate or drank in the last twenty-four hours. Did you eat something because you were nervous, tired, or stressed? Did you need to sneak a chocolate bar or potato chips for some quick energy just to make it until lunch or dinner? If you said yes, don't panic. There is still time to change your eating habits and turn yourself into a healthy mom. If you said no, then you are well on your way to optimizing your body's energy.

HELPING YOUR BODY DIGEST FOOD

It is better for your digestive system to consume four to six smaller meals a day versus three big ones. As your pregnancy advances, your stomach becomes compressed by your growing baby and cannot hold as much food as it did in the past. Your small and large intestines snake around your uterus, making digestion take longer than before.

Help your digestive system manage all of these changes by eating smaller quantities of food more often. Also, avoid things that may take a long time to digest. You will know what foods your body has difficulty digesting. They are the ones that often come back up into your esophagus as heartburn.

This is something that many women need support and encouragement to accomplish. Right now, the industry of weight loss products and services nets $33 billion a year. Images and ideas of a "perfect" size assault women everywhere and often suggest that pregnant mothers are too big, even if their increase in size is due to pregnancy.

Optimizing your body's energy is about more than just body size; it is about nutritious eating designed to increase your natural strength and longevity.

Unfortunately, eating healthy is something that many women have difficulty achieving. Many women have jobs or family demands that force them to eat out or grab a quick snack. If this is your situation too, cut back on takeout and hastily thrown together meals. Restructure your time so that eating becomes an act of nourishing your body.

If time is something you are lacking, plan ahead. Here's a practical doula timesaving food tip: Make snacks of dried fruit and fresh vegetables like papayas and carrots that you can munch on during the day. You can even prepare a number of them and store them in the pantry or the fridge in small plastic bags. Simply drop a bag into your purse, backpack, or pocket for an instant healthy snack.

Another idea? Shorten your food preparation by making stews, casseroles, and other one-pot meals that you can put together in minutes. Crockpots may be a throwback to your mom's era, but they make things simpler in the kitchen. For more simple, nutritious food ideas, spend some time in your local library or bookstore's food section. There are a number of excellent cookbooks on this subject that you can purchase or borrow for your kitchen.

If you are like most women, what to eat is just as concerning as how much to eat. Don't worry. You are not alone in thinking that food is supposed to come supersized.

REGULAR SERVING SIZES

You've heard people refer to a serving size, but I bet you couldn't identify one. If you think a meal of roasted chicken and a

Table 2.1   Food Groups

Food Group	*Example of One Serving*	
Grains	Bread	1 slice
	Cooked rice or pasta	$^1/_2$ Cup
Vegetables	Raw leafy vegetables	1 Cup
	Other cooked or raw vegetables	$^1/_2$ Cup
Fruit	Banana	1 medium
	Fresh, cooked, or canned fruit	$^1/_2$ Cup
Dairy	Milk	1 Cup
	Natural cheese	$1^1/_2$ oz.
Meats, beans, nuts	Cooked lean meat	2–3 oz.
	Eggs	1 entire egg

side of rice constitutes two servings—one of chicken, the other of rice—you are mistaken. Serving sizes are based on food quantity and weight.

Table 2.1 has two examples of one serving from each of the five food groups. Pay attention to the amount that is considered one serving of each item listed.

Looking at this list carefully, you will notice some important information about food intake. According to my chart, an entire banana is one serving. The food guide pyramid found on most grocery products says that you need two to three servings of fruit a day. To achieve this serving requirement, you only need to have a banana with lunch and one-half cup of unsweetened applesauce after dinner. Simple and nutritious.

That is also the goal of a new national campaign that hopes to make healthy eating simpler to accomplish. It is called Five a Day and encourages people to do just that: eat five fruits and vegetables every day.

Just as with the banana and applesauce trick mentioned above, this is also easy to do.

✓ Add papaya (excellent for aiding digestion of other foods), cantaloupes, mangoes, and grapefruit to your diet as light desserts.

✓ Eat natural (no extra butter, no extra salt) popcorn during the day when you have a hunger craving.

✓ Add vegetables to your diet by preparing them in a variety of ways. You can eat them raw, steamed, or grilled.

✓ Some pregnant mothers have to feed their children as well as themselves. What are some ways to add fruits and vegetables to meals that everyone will enjoy? Here are some quick doula tips:

✓ Grill vegetables in slices that can be added to salads as strips and sandwiches as "pickles."

✓ Place an entire vegetable, like an eggplant, under the broiler. Turn it over occasionally, making sure that it doesn't burn. Once the insides are soft, take it out of the oven. You can test this by poking the vegetable with a knife and seeing if the knife moves smoothly through the pulp. Peel the skin off and discard, chop up the pulp, and blend for an instant sauce that can be added to pasta or rice.

These are some of the quick tips that I recommend to moms. You can create more by simply experimenting in the kitchen. The more confidence you have in preparing meals the more creative you can be!

Now that you understand more about serving sizes and creative ways to reach five fruits and vegetables a day, you may be wondering how to know you are getting the required vitamins and minerals your baby needs. Although many moms, including you, are taking prenatal supplements, you should still eat foods rich in nutrients. Your prenatal supplement does not take the place of a healthy diet. So what foods can help you and your baby remain strong?

I have created a chart (Table 2.2) that gives at least one good food source for each nutrient listed in the Recommended Daily Allowances chart created by the Food Nutrition Board of the National Research Council. The RDA chart is an excellent resource that aims to educate pregnant women about the appropriate levels of dietary nutrients needed each day. My addition makes it plain what food sources help you to achieve these recommendations.

As you can see from this chart, there are many food options that can help you meet your dietary requirements. What is the difference between a milligram and a microgram? Plenty. But that is information I will let you obtain from your doctor, midwife, or dietitian. As a doula, I am interested in encouraging healthy living by explaining how easy it is to achieve.

The information here is only the first step in empowering yourself about your body. You may have cravings that are messages from your body that something is missing. These details only become known if you educate yourself and seek help from the professionals who can provide you with more information so you can go one step further in your mission of optimizing your pregnant body. Make healthy eating part of your overall mission to achieve wellness for the rest of your life, not just the months of pregnancy.

GETTING ENOUGH TO DRINK

Sodas and even some supposed fruit drinks are loaded with sugar. This can translate to increased calories without increased nutrient intake. Omit sodas and other sweetened drinks from your diet. Instead, drink milk, water, pure fruit juice, and decaffeinated, unsweetened tea. These beverages will help you consume the eight glasses of liquid you need each day without the extra sugar that you don't need.

Table 2.2   Recommended Daily Allowances with
Suggested Sources

Vitamin A	Liver
Vitamin D	Fatty fish
Vitamin E	Wheat germ
Vitamin K	Dark green leafy vegetables
Vitamin C	Strawberries
Thiamin—Vitamin B_1	Whole grains
Riboflavin—Vitamin B_2	Salmon
Niacin	Peanut butter
Vitamin B_6	Chicken
Folate	Dark green leafy vegetables
Vitamin B_{12}	Meat
Calcium	Low-fat milk products
Phosphorus	Dairy products and grains
Magnesium	Low-fat milk
Iron	Lean meat
Zinc	Lean meat
Iodine	Salt that has been enriched with iodine
Selenium	Brazil nuts and meat

A quick doula tip: Fill a recycled two and a half quart plastic jug with water each day and place it in your refrigerator at home or at work. Drink from it all day until it is empty. This way you do not have to worry about counting the number of remaining glasses needed to reach the required amount. When you finish the jug, you have met your fluid requirement for the day.

But don't stop there. A healthy lifestyle is composed of nutrition and movement. Many people think of exercise as vigorous motions done in a gym. True exercise is defined simply as activity that enhances blood flow and releases stress. From swimming to prenatal aerobics to walking, options for keeping your pregnant body fit abound.

And the benefits may be more than just enhanced blood flow. Studies show that a moderate exercise program shortens the time a mom is in labor and the length of her postpartum recovery period. If you exercise, make sure that you talk to your practitioner about the safety of your particular activity.

While mothers in the past were warned not to exercise during pregnancy, mothers today hear a whole new tune. The most recent ACOG (American College of Obstetricians and Gynecologists) recommendations for exercise during pregnancy ask that women do the following:

✓ Exercise at least three times a week

✓ Skip exercising when sick

✓ Exercise in comfortable clothing and surroundings

✓ Warm up and cool down after each activity

✓ Take an accurate count of their heartbeat to keep it below 150 beats per minute

✓ Drink lots of water before, during, and after the activity

✓ Stop exercising when uncomfortable

✓ Avoid being on their backs

Do not start a new exercise during the latter months of pregnancy. If you are curious what would be an appropriate, gentle activity for you, consult your doctor or midwife.

STAYING AWAY FROM DANGEROUS CHEMICALS

I know I don't have to remind you, but it never hurts to repeat it: Keep up your determination to avoid cigarettes, alcohol, caffeine, and other chemicals. Much is known about the effects of drugs and alcohol, but little attention is given to paints, cleaning products, and other chemicals used in a variety of professions and home improvement projects.

If you are concerned about any chemicals that you encounter on your job, talk to your supervisor and your doctor or midwife about its safety.

Some household chemicals state on the packaging that they may not be safe for inhalation or use by pregnant women. Read the packaging of any product before you use it and consult your practitioner about any questions you may have.

A healthy mom who wants to live naturally, in balance with her environment, needs to be a smart one.

There are certain medical conditions that make exercise an unsafe option for a pregnant mother experiencing them, things like high blood pressure, heart disease, vaginal bleeding, and premature labor or contractions.

You should also stop exercising immediately and contact your doctor or midwife if you experience dizziness, cramping, pain, bleeding, or an extremely elevated heart rate.

Dancing, singing, walking, yoga, prenatal aerobics, and swimming are just some of the many things you can do to move your body. Not only will your body respond positively to movement, but so too will your spirit.

Your holistic journey of pregnancy depends on a comprehensive approach to living that sees the various parts of you existing as a whole. We have already covered your pregnant mind and body. Our final examination will be your pregnant spirit.

Your spirit, something that means many things to many people, plays an integral part in your conscious experience of pregnancy. The next chapter presents information to help strengthen your spirit while adding positive energy to your life.

3

❄ ❄ ❄

YOUR PREGNANT SPIRIT

Within every person is a spirit. Some people define spirit as a vital force or essence of themselves, something intangible yet essential to existing. Others see spirit as an actual energy force—something that interacts with the various elements on earth, fluctuating and adapting its essence in response to pain, happiness, growth, and uncertainty.

For our purposes, spirit means all these things and more. It can have a religious element or be essentially natural. How it came to be is immaterial. The only important understanding of spirit that I am concentrating on is its existence as a part of you.

As a pregnant mother, you have a spirit, an essence that is altering and changing as you journey through motherhood. The many physical and mental changes that you go through transform your spirit. It is here that negative thoughts about your body, fears about your partner, and concerns about motherhood can take root and slowly eat at you. This can wound or strain your spirit. The spirit can also soar and take flight from the positive energy and renewal you feed it, keeping the essence of yourself whole and complete.

Some women renew and sustain their spirit by attending religious gatherings or reading spiritual words that can sustain their faith and their oneness with the world. Other mothers engage in uplifting activities that provide them with a wellspring of positive energy.

I strive to bring positive energy and renewal of spirit into my life on a continuous basis. I know how important it is that I stay renewed. If I do not take care of myself, how can I help nurture and sustain someone else?

Positive energy channeled into a mother's spirit can change every facet of her life. In many ways, this is the kind of energy that a doula brings to a birth. She offers support to a mother that maybe, just maybe, allows that mom to tap into the positive energy within herself. And mothers need it in our world today.

Studies show that many mothers are in a time bind, struggling to be everything in a world that demands more. They want to give more and be more, but often have little left over after doing what they feel they have to do to keep everything in their lives afloat.

This kind of "I have to do everything for everybody" approach is spiritually draining. It is, unfortunately, the only way that many mothers know.

Over the years, I have made notes to myself about how to increase my energy as a doula and have collected tips about positive mothering. It's interesting that these two lists are nearly identical. Perhaps living a positive, energy-filled life is something every woman needs.

To get you started on your journey of living positively during your pregnancy, I have prepared ten tips to renew your spirit and your life.

I can't guarantee that these tips will solve every personal problem or concern that you have. What I can state is that they are so simple and easy—and the benefits so immense—that you will ask yourself why you never tried these things sooner. To help remind you of your positive-living pledge, each tip comes with an affirmation exercise to help you maintain positive energy in your life.

TEN EASY WAYS TO INFUSE YOUR SOUL WITH POSITIVE ENERGY

1. Greet Each Day with Joy

Each breath that you take, each sunrise that you see is one that you will never see again. It is a gift to you, one that reminds you of the blessing of each day.

You too have been blessed. You are a mother. Within you is the child who will change you and your life in many ways.

This is something to remember every day. Starting tomorrow, wake with joy in your every breath and thankfulness in your spirit at the blessing of a child. Amazingly, difficulties will appear surmountable and happiness more abundant. Joy is something to greet each day with. Awake in the morning and smile. Few things in the world are as infectious as a smile. It fills your entire being and actually creeps into your soul.

Once you have smiled, take a moment to welcome that day. Many women do this already in their own special way. I enjoy watching the sky change from my bed and reflecting on my family. This quiet moment allows me to start my day in the right frame of mind—focusing on positive rather than negative things. Waking up this way affects my entire day. I am centered and happy, rather than troubled and stressed, as I go out into the world.

What is your greeting? Create an affirmation that expresses your commitment to welcoming each day with joy. Use terms that are positive in nature and doable in your life. Words like "can," "will," and "need" allow you to state in real language the way that you will respond to this situation when you face it again.

Start three sentences with "I can," "I will," and "Just for me, I need to." Finish each sentence with a statement of truth for greeting each day with joy.

2. Be Thankful

Oprah Winfrey started something a number of years ago with her idea of gratitude journals. Since then, she and others have encouraged millions of women to be thankful for the many things in their lives. I believe that this kind of thankfulness has powerful ramifications. By recognizing the good things in our lives, we deprive the negative aspects of the ability to cause pain or stress.

A good friend of mine who has a child with special needs often remarks about how joyful her child appears every morning. This child seems to know that this is another day of life and is thankful for it.

Look at your life now. What things are you thankful for? Your baby? Your partner? Your family? Home?

Consider the most basic needs in your life. Are these being met? Acknowledge that. Are there things that you still desire? Recognize them, and either strive to bring them into your life or release the desire. Even with unmet needs, acknowledge all that you have and give thanks for everything.

As a doula, I try to remain focused on the thankful aspects of a birth. I often thank the medical staff for working with me. I thank a mother and her partner for trusting me enough to allow me to enter this time of birth with them. I also thank their baby for allowing me to share the moment of his or her birth. I recognize that I am blessed to be in a profession that can have such a positive impact on families.

Remind yourself why you should be thankful with an affirmation to help you meet your goal.

3. Rest When You Feel Tired

Being pregnant is hard work. Within you, hormonal and biological changes are altering your body every day. Some changes are internal, quiet occurrences, whereas others are noticeable the moment they happen. No wonder you are tired at the end of each day.

Some moms are amazed at their lack of energy during the latter months of their pregnancies. They felt invigorated during the middle months of pregnancy, only to find their energy level dropping during their seventh and eighth months. During this time, a mother's body is working hard to finish the job of growing a healthy baby.

Do not take on more obligations than you can handle at this time and wear yourself out. Repeat after me: If I feel tired, I will take it easy.

Many mothers convince themselves that they cannot rest because of chores, dinner, and other responsibilities. These things are important, but so is growing a healthy baby. A well-rested, strong mother goes into labor with more energy and stamina than a sleep-deprived, tired mother who may feel even more pain and discomfort as a result of her fatigued body. Take the time now to give your body rest when you need it.

If you have young children, exchange baby-sitting with a mother who lives near you. This way the two of you can alternate breaks while providing your children with playmates and an adult to supervise them. If you are still working, take power naps during your lunch break. A five-minute nap with your feet up on a stool, chair, or even a pile of books can do wonders for your spirit and your mind.

If you can afford it, arrange to have a qualified child care person take your other children out of the house so that you can sleep undisturbed. You can also find some quiet time with the help of your partner. This is the person who is your other half. Let him share in the child-raising duties that you have both assumed.

If the baby within you is your first, create time for renewal. Whether you start your day peacefully or end it with a power nap, rest whenever you can.

There are a couple of simple things that you can do at work to help you feel rejuvenated. First, invest in some disposable wet washcloths that you can use to wipe your face for instant freshness. This can give you the illusion of a shower when you feel taxed and tired at work. The next couple of things depend on your work environment. If you are at a desk, consider obtaining a small step stool that you can place your feet on. This will help with circulation. You can also place lumbar support pillows in your chair if you have to do prolonged sitting.

No matter what you do, recognize your needs during this time and rest whenever you can.

State an affirmation, an honest and realistic one, to claim rest when you need it.

4. Believe in Yourself

Believing in yourself is one of the surest ways to fulfill your dreams, conquer your fears, and bolster your spirit. Doulas believe in themselves every time they are with a mother. They do not believe that they can perform miracles or force anything to happen that shouldn't. They simply offer services and skills that they trust will help and comfort a mother in some small way. Scientific studies may reinforce this benefit, but doulas also know in their hearts that their work is important. I often hear doulas say that doula work comes from the heart.

You too will find that believing in yourself, as a mother, will stimulate many areas of your life. Your strength, your dreams, your courage, and your hope for yourself and your family are all affected by your beliefs.

You need an affirmation that will help you deal with this topic head-on in order to help you achieve your goal. Create a statement that resonates truth yet remains positive.

5. Laugh Often

So much in life is simply funny. Even the most frustrating moments can disclose a hidden gem of ironic humor or comedic insanity—all you can do is laugh. Pregnancy is one of those times when laughter can be an ally.

While clinical descriptions explain the changes that occur during the months of pregnancy, there are times when even the best words cannot express the amazing occurrence of bearing a new life. Look at your own life. You are probably in your later months of pregnancy. What has it been like so far? Can you believe the size of your breasts? What about your uterus, seemingly stretching like a balloon?

Many mothers are unprepared for the fast-moving physical experience of pregnancy. Rather than battle the changes, accept them. They have to happen in order for your baby to grow.

Yet embracing these changes will only allow you to see them as something that has to happen. I want you to go one step further. I want you to see them as things that are surreal and beautiful at the same time. How do you do this? Laugh.

No man will ever experience the surprising movements of a baby inside of him, the surreal feeling of heartburn at 3:00 A.M., or the pressure of a baby's head during the final weeks of pregnancy that feels as if a small ball is going to drop out at any moment. No man can experience this transformation because only women like you produce babies; women who are strong, confident, and hopefully amused.

Have you ever heard the adage that you attract more bees with honey than with vinegar? Well, there's another one. You can bear anything with a good joke. And this isn't just strange doula folk wisdom. According to the Association for Applied and Therapeutic Humor, scientific research studies suggest that laughter creates physiological changes in the body that seem to increase tolerance of pain and lower the body's production of stress hormones. Their wise definition of therapeutic humor is any intervention that promotes health and wellness by stimulating a playful discovery, expression, or appreciation of the absurdity or incongruity of life's situations. What they are implying is that the old adage "laughter is the best medicine" may hold more truth than we ever imagined.

Create a statement for yourself that will help you bring more laughter into your life.

6. Ask for Help When You Need It

Television shows abound with images of supermom. Earlier shows like *Leave It to Beaver* and *The Brady Bunch* had models of mothers who never struggled with how to manage their home or raise their family. These women seemed to have no self-doubts, stress, or anxiety.

Shows today present a more realistic woman, but rarely do they display the need that every mother has for assistance in raising her children.

Husbands, fathers, grandparents, partners, other relatives, and friends are all important members of a baby's life. And now, during your pregnancy, is the time to cultivate these relationships and tell these people what you need from them.

You know the old saying, "It takes a village to raise a child"? Well, it takes more than a village; it takes loving people who are willing to help and love babies throughout their infancy and into adulthood.

Susan Hrdy, a noted researcher and scientist, describes in her book, *Mother Nature,* what she calls alloparents. According to Hrdy, alloparents are all the individuals besides the mother and father who assist in raising a baby.

Alloparents are not just isolated people who help with babies. Alloparents represent a community approach to living and existing as concerned members of a whole. In many ways, we are all responsible for the inhabitants of this planet, forever linked into a wide network of alloparents, allo-friends, and allo-communities.

Search in your family and community for alloparents for your baby. The community approach to raising a baby will have amazing effects on you. It is much easier to give love and support to your baby when you are receiving support and love yourself.

Remind yourself of these connections often as you seek to create a balanced and positive life.

7. *Express Your Emotions*

Being a doula is like walking around in heightened states of emotion. Staying in tune with a mother's needs and her family's, working well with a doctor or midwife, and keeping the nursing staff well assured of their value, along with a partner's, can take its toll emotionally. I help express my emotions by carrying a small pad of paper to record my emotional state after a birth. I try to capture my true feelings about everything without censoring myself or holding back.

An amazing thing happens when I do this. By releasing my thoughts in a private place, I am emotionally lighter and clearer about my thoughts.

You need to let your emotions out too. Have you expressed your fears, concerns, and questions about becoming a mother? Who has heard your ideas about birth?

You can talk to a doula, but she is only one of the many people who would welcome a discussion with you. Do not overlook your partner, your parents, a respected person from your community, or even your doctor or midwife as potential sounding boards.

Expressing your emotions with someone you trust and in a journal are only two ways of letting your feelings out.

Create artwork. Some mothers find their artistic vein is fueled by the life teeming within them. Let your creative energies soar as you tap a vital part of your spirit. Do something simple like playing with clay. Quilt. Paint. (Use nontoxic paint products to protect your baby.) Draw. Create something just for your baby such as a keepsake journal. Many kits are available at card shops.

Write letters. Parents, partners, and kids love to read letters meant only for them. Write your baby about this time of pregnancy and place it in his or her baby album. Give a letter to a partner or a parent that catalogues and expresses your impressions of becoming a mother. Sometimes this kind of letter sharing may be just the connection that is needed to bring a mother (you) closer to her own parents.

Sometimes expressing emotions turns up information or issues that you aren't prepared to handle on your own. If you feel that you would like to have a deeper discussion with a partner or relative, please seek out someone who has experience with family counseling.

Although counseling has become a routine concept for many people, most do not understand its significance in relation to helping someone become a whole, complete person. Emotional baggage that is intense can become a major issue during pregnancy. A series of studies published in the *British Medical Journal* states that depression during pregnancy may be even more common than depression and the "baby blues" after birth.

This is something that is rarely discussed in pregnancy books and in childbirth classes. And that needs to change.

Seek help if you feel any of these symptoms: problems with concentrating, problems with sleeping, fatigue, changes in eating habits, anxiety, irritability, or blue feelings. Some of these are symptoms of pregnancy and may be hard to discern from true depression. If you are concerned, talk to your doctor or midwife.

No matter what you are feeling, consider an affirmation that lets you constructively and honestly release your emotions.

8. Live More, Organize Less

Many mothers work hard to have an efficient home and raise cultured, intelligent children. Surprisingly, they attempt to accomplish this by completing a long list of things every day. Clean often. Cook quick meals. Chauffeur their children to a variety of after-school and weekend activities. Parents who cannot afford this type of lifestyle often believe their family suffers because they are unable to offer it to them.

Time issues motivate much of this kind of living. Mothers want more of it so that they can get more done.

Arlie Hochschild, a respected sociologist, wrote an interesting book on this dilemma called *The Time Bind.* She discusses the bind that mothers and fathers find themselves in as they struggle to be and do everything.

E-mail. PDAs. On-line banking. Twenty-four-hour day care. On-line grocery shopping. All of these time savers keep many of us tied to the myth of the organized, efficient mother.

With more and more pregnant mothers working, this need for speed at work and at home can be physically, mentally, and spiritually draining. Even mothers who work within the home, both literally and figuratively, find it difficult to make time for themselves or their families.

This is no way to live and experience the richness of life. Unfortunately, it affects too many women. More mothers need to learn ways to live more and organize less while breaking the bind that keeps them from living the life that they seek for their babies, their families, and themselves.

Although technology and other time savers can make life less stressful, they can also restrict us from feeling life in a sensorially rich, spiritually empowering way. Pregnancy is a time to use your senses to see, hear, smell, touch, and taste the many changes all around you. This becomes harder and harder to do as we become more detached from sensing life.

Take time today for a quiet cup of juice when the house is quiet. Taste the natural sweetness within the liquid. Let the flavor settle in your mouth and dance across your tongue.

Play Frisbee in your garden or rent a funny movie. Laugh and sing out loud without worrying whether you look or sound crazy. Talk to people who enrich your life just by being with you.

Smell the many flowers that grow throughout the year in your area. Take moments to do whatever strikes you at this time in your life. Simply live.

By running around, organizing and tending to endless details, you may force your spirit to miss out on the joy of living. This detachment can ultimately cause you to feel like you are running on empty, going through the motions of caring for yourself and your family but not actually experiencing anything. You can't live this way for long. Eventually, little cracks develop in your soul that break open and completely overpower everything. Existing from day to day like this is akin to being spiritually dead.

You deserve to live every day of your life to the fullest. I would encourage you to abandon every time saver you own, but that advice would be neither practical nor helpful. Why? Many mothers like their time savers. Instead of asking you to abandon them, I want you to look for ways to infuse your life with simplicity from the inside out so that you can experience the world as a fuller, brighter place:

Take a holiday from your television. Turn off your TV and enjoy your partner and your growing baby. Television shows and movies are wonderful entertainment options, but they can limit your interaction with people around you.

Recognize the benefits and the disconnectedness of technology. The twenty-first century is a time teeming with technological breakthroughs and advances that enable many of us to do more things with greater perceived organization and increased efficiency. Some of these benefits are illusory. How much we do is not measured in a finite chart. Ultimately, we want more; any advances we create are immediately thrust aside for the next thing that will allow us to move faster.

Embrace technology for its good, but recognize this: life isn't necessarily better because you can complete things more quickly.

Set time aside to do nothing.   It is tempting to plan every moment of the day with activities. Work. Play. Lunch dates. More work. Life moves fast enough without adding more items onto the to-do list.

What you need is time to do nothing. Put everything to the side and simply breathe. Your mini-vacation can include a warm bath, a quiet stroll in your neighborhood, or even an ice cream cone in the park. Give yourself the freedom to do absolutely nothing for as long as you like.

Give yourself an affirmation to enable you to have a lived life rather than a better organized one.

9. *Try Not to Overextend Yourself*

I can recall one month, early in my doula career, when I had a number of clients due around the same time, a child's birthday, and demands from organizations that stretched me thinner than I wanted. I gave of myself to everyone and everything, and then at the end of the month, collapsed in exhaustion. I pledged right then to never put myself in that position again. I learned not to overextend myself. It saps me mentally and spiritually.

Now I simply take on what I can do well without stretching myself too thin, politely turning down everything I can't. I also have made friends with the word "no." It is important for me to embrace what I can do, and do well, and pass on the things that I simply cannot handle without weakening all of my efforts.

I try to make my family a priority and my sanity, spirituality, and strength a necessity. It has taken me a long time to learn this lesson. Why? Because I am like many of you in thinking that I am good at multitasking.

We women have gotten better and better at saying that we are not overextended; we are good at juggling fifteen things at the same time. In truth, you might be able to make it work. But there's a catch to this juggle-fest. The laws of science say that you will occasionally drop one of the balls that you juggle so well. The scary part is that you do not know which ball it will be.

Strive right now to stop juggling things—doing more simply for the sake of trying to get more done. You are only one person, one spiritually exhausted person if you continue doing it all.

This is a lesson to learn now during your pregnancy, when you need to draw your strength around you in order to bring a healthy baby into the world.

To remember this, you need a serious pledge to fully meet this goal. Why? It is hard not to want to do everything and help everyone in your life. The truth is you won't help anyone, including your baby, by giving so much of yourself to everyone that you have nothing left for yourself. And without a base of sanity and strength at the core of your spirit, it gets harder and harder to continue to love and nurture others.

10. Surround Yourself with Love

Watching a mother and her partner stare at their beautiful creation moments after birth is a wondrous gift. I have the privilege as a doula to share an intimate, blessed moment with families.

But babies aren't the only ones who thrive when surrounded by positive energy and loving people. Mothers and fathers also benefit from giving and receiving such powerful emotions. By keeping and filling a well full of love, parents are thus able to give it from an overflowing source to each other and their baby.

What kind of love am I talking about? Love between relatives. Love among friends. Love between parents. And even love of oneself. All of these types of love are important. If you don't feel as if you are getting love from any of these sources, work on changing that.

You can start by reflecting on yourself first. Do you believe in yourself in all aspects of life, including motherhood? Hopefully, you said yes. If not, then make building your self-esteem and self-confidence a top priority. A number of books are currently available that can help women gain this in their lives. Search for relevant titles at your local bookstore or library.

The relationship with your partner and your family may be harder to strengthen, since this typically involves a committed effort from all parties involved to enact change.

Before you venture into a complicated attempt at relationship and love rebuilding between yourself, your partner, and/or your family, test the receptiveness of the other parties involved. Try to ascertain the willingness of everyone to strengthen the love that connects each person to the other. This can be done in a letter or as a discussion.

From there, your options are open. Counseling from a professional is a possibility. Professional therapists or counselors are trained to assist partners and families who are choosing to work together on their relationships, even through difficult situations. You can also arrange for another family member or a friend to act as an intermediary to assist with any reconciliation.

Of course, you also have the option of doing nothing for the time being. As much as I am a champion of love, I am also a realist. Some situations are best left until all parties, including you, are ready to change them. You may not be ready for this type of emotional work, so don't force it on yourself.

Instead, develop a plan of contact and sharing that keeps positive communication going until a date in the future when you may be spiritually ready for healing.

Although all of these tips can help you in your relationships, the best way to begin surrounding yourself with love is to think it, feel it, and express it in your everyday life. Lenny Kravitz has a song that is emblematic of this: "Let Love Rule." That is your final tip to bring positive energy into your life. Let love rule your life and give your spirit the added strength to help you sustain yourself and your family.

These ten tips to creating and sustaining positive energy in your life can help you tackle life with more confidence and renewed spiritual strength. Yet sustaining your mind, body, and spirit begins with you believing that you are important. Once you believe that, revitalizing and nurturing yourself and your family becomes easier to do.

Your pregnancy is a special time that enables you to focus your energy on many aspects of your life as your body grows your baby. However, there will come a time, if you aren't already there, when your thoughts and even your dreams become consumed with your baby's birth.

Women who have reached this point in their pregnancies often become voracious readers of everything that details how birth happens. They can fear the unknown of birth and maybe even wonder how they are going to go through "it" with confidence and strength.

These types of concerns can weaken a mother's awareness of and connection to her baby throughout birth. Birth, the transformative moment where one's baby comes literally through one's body, is a time when the mind, body, and spirit connection is at its highest.

The next chapters cover the philosophy of birth, the various places where birth can occur, and the many ways a mother can comfort and enrich her experience of this moment. Nothing is spared in this discussion; including epidurals, cesareans, and the experience of birth through the partner's eyes.

The birth of your baby deserves to be a moment that you experience completely within your mind, body, and spirit.

Part Two

❋ ❋ ❋

EMBRACING CHILDBIRTH

What exactly is birth? Everyone has ideas about this. Medical dictionaries call birth the act of expelling a baby from the womb. A number of health texts refer to it as an event that announces the end of pregnancy. The late columnist and writer Erma Bombeck once said that at her child's birth, she got a shot in the hip and awoke from the effects of the medication when her child went to school. All of these descriptions, no matter their intent, lack something.

Listen to the feeling behind this account of birth from *Our Bodies, Ourselves for the New Century:* "Some women feel that time stops and all their energy leaves them as they gaze in wonder at their newborn . . . but birth is the continuation of a process that began with conception. Your connection is already intimate" (p. 478). This passage starts to put into words the miraculous and emotionally gripping moment that is birth.

Read birth stories. They present gripping details of the emotional intensity that characterizes the first moments of a new family. Some birth stories are mostly compilations of scattered memories. The experience so transcends normal time that many mothers lose track of hours or even days. Nevertheless, their feelings during the moment stay with them.

Some moms react emotionally to their child's birth years later as if it had just occurred.

How would you like your baby to be born? In what kind of environment? Where would you like your partner to be when your baby makes his first entrance into the world? Beside you? With his hands joined with yours to pull your baby onto your warm chest? What kind of technology do you want or not want offered to you?

All of these questions and more are part of the magic and the mystery of birth. However, these ideas are not just concepts to think about during the hours of labor and birth. Women who report feeling strong and nurtured during their baby's birth, no matter the actual process, store the confidence that surged through them and see the world differently. After experiencing such an event, they "feel" transformed as a mother and as a woman.

Cultures around the world recognize the transformation of birth, often renaming a mother and a father after they have been through the process. Our society has no process in place to recognize this event as the holistic moment it is. Naming ceremonies, where the baby is formally named in front of family and friends, exist, as do other welcoming parties. However, most of these, including showers, are geared toward the new baby.

Your baby will irrevocably change both you and your partner. Her presence in your life will be like a birth into a new role in life.

For now, consider what memories you will store from this event. In addition, how will your mind, body, and spirit engage fully in the moment?

The chapters in Part 2 will aid you on this journey of discovery. Although they are not divided into the mind, body, and spirit of birth, these concepts are embedded deeply in every chapter, as I want this moment to remain a holistic event. Holistic birth, though, is much more than just an ideal; it is a way of witnessing and experiencing birth as a sacred moment.

I hope this information prepares you to embrace all of the wonder that birth brings.

4

✤ ✤ ✤

BIRTH PHILOSOPHY

Mothers have their own varied ideas about birth. Some mothers want a more natural birth experience, free of medication and intervention. Other moms are seeking a balance of medical pain relief and awareness, preferring not to rule out any options for the safety of their baby.

Although many moms have this "wait and see" attitude, I find that most want to experience the birth of their baby in a particular manner. They envision certain events occurring and base these goals on a particular birth philosophy.

A birth philosophy consists of the combined goals, hopes, ideals, and thoughts about birth that draw together concepts about the formation of families, the role of practitioners, and the power of women. An example of a birth philosophy in action is placing a newly born baby in contact with its mother's stomach or chest. Facilitating bonding would be the goal in this instance, something many mothers and their partners feel is critical in the first moments after birth.

Another example of a birth philosophy is when a father cuts his baby's umbilical cord, officially removing the baby from her dependency on the placenta and placing her within the world of her family. This symbolic act of union is one many fathers enact as a gesture of their role as half the parenting team in their baby's life. This birth philosophy embraces partnership and togetherness.

I see these and other birth philosophies played out time and again during birth as mothers choose to dance, sing, groan loudly, sit against their partners during pushing, and give birth standing with their arms around their partner's neck.

A birth philosophy is a personal testimony to your thoughts and feelings as a woman, and your belief and confidence in your ability to give birth. Some mothers embrace their strength but recognize the place of medicine within their concept of birth. This is still a legitimate birth philosophy. Knowing what you believe about birth will enable you to understand how you and others will work through it.

What is your philosophy about birth? What goals do you have in mind for yourself, your partner, or your baby? What about your doctor or midwife's goals?

Just as you have a birth philosophy, so too does your practitioner. I have found that some of the thorniest disagreements between a mother and a practitioner occur because they have different philosophies of birth. One may prefer that birth occur in a natural pattern while the other may support technology-assisted labor and birth. Talk to your doctor or midwife now so that you are aware of his or her birth philosophy and can plan ways that your entire birth team (your partner, doula, and others) can work together to provide specific assistance to you.

Your practitioner, though, has to work in a birth environment that also has its own philosophy (excluding homebirths). Practitioners who need to keep their privileges to see clients at certain hospitals or birth centers sometimes have to adjust their birth philosophy in order to continue working at a certain facility. This may make them struggle with concepts or procedures that they would freely reject without the pressure to adopt the same ideals as the birth facility.

Some practitioners have gone so far as to stop working in environments that have birth philosophies they find unacceptable. Amazingly, mothers have done the same thing. They have elected not to give birth in places that cling to outdated birth philosophies. This consumer charge has created amazing changes, especially in hospitals.

HOSPITALS

Hospitals are as varied as the cities they are housed in. Some are more like spas that offer healing, while others are more utilitarian in look and use. Trying to outline a typical hospital scenario is like trying to guess the various flavors in a rainbow smoothie: some things may be recognizable; others may not. To simplify our discussion, I will present what generally happens during a hospital birth and explain how you can navigate your way within the environment.

The first thing I want you to consider about hospitals is how you feel about them. Many people believe that hospitals are institutions for sick people. In fact, for centuries, childbearing women gave birth at home, far removed from any formal building. The maternity wards and hospitals that eventually sprang up were created to offer services to poor women. As time went by, they became increasingly popular as technological interventions during birth also increased. Unfortunately, health outcomes in hospitals didn't benefit from the increase in technology. The procedures continued because many became part of the accepted routine of managing birth in the hospital.

Today, hospitals have improved their negative image; premiere teaching and learning institutions offer services to paying and nonpaying mothers alike. Many hospitals, though, continue to envision birth as a medical event that needs managing.

Fortunately, there are some alternatives to this approach. *US News and World Report* recently presented its twelfth annual America's Best Hospitals survey. It analyzed 6,116 hospitals that, at the time of the survey, were affiliated with a medical school, a member of the Council of Teaching Hospitals, or a facility that offered a large list of technological services.

Searching among this survey for the top pregnancy- and birth-related sites reveals places like Brigham and Women's Hospital in Boston. This prestigious hospital evolved over the years as multiple area hospitals merged. Within its current system is the Mary Horrigan Connors Center for Women's Health. Its maternity wing has comfortable birthing suites, private rooms, rocking chairs, twenty-four-hour room service, and valet parking for partners at the hospital's main entrance. Color and comfort are in every detail. Amazingly, it resembles a four-star hotel rather than a hospital.

Is this hospital a rarity? Yes and no. There are hospitals that will never have the financial resources to offer maternity services similar to Brigham and Women's. Your hospital might be such a place. Yet from coast to coast, hospitals throughout the United States are creating maternity services that are family focused and mother and baby friendly. It is becoming increasingly common to find breast-feeding counselors and intrahospital television stations broadcasting twenty-four-hour baby care tips. Nurseries have been abandoned in favor of a mother and her baby staying together in many postpartum floors.

But something else is also common. Statistically, mothers who give birth in a hospital can expect to undergo a number of procedures as routine protocol. While outdated customs, like shaving a mother's pubic hair for a vaginal birth or performing enemas have been abandoned, other procedures like intermittent or continuous electronic fetal monitoring have become standard practice. And the list of procedures doesn't stop there. As of this writing, about 22 percent of all births end up as cesarean sections. In some hospitals, this number is dramatically higher.

Statistics, though, are just numbers. They give no indication how your birth will occur with your practitioner, your partner, or your doula in attendance—not to mention your baby.

Although all of these numbers may sound like your birth experience has already been decided for you, it really hasn't. If a hospital birth is in your future, you can give birth holistically within it. How do you do that, given the statistics that you face and the complexity of the system?

Hospitals are like any other institution. Some people are in charge, and others assist those who are in charge. Some people work behind the scenes to keep the ship running, and others are at the forefront, right in the middle of the action. Recognize who has power and who doesn't from the moment you enter the building. This will save you from doing things like asking the housekeeping staff if you can get something to eat.

Be forewarned: When you enter the hospital, your identity folds into the goals of the institution. Hospitals strive to deliver babies who are healthy in a timely manner. They achieve this by doing a plethora of medical procedures they consider essential to the birth of a healthy baby. Some of these procedures seem counter to the idea of holism. How can you navigate this kind of system and claim a holistic birth?

Start by recognizing that your hospital may be similar to other places, but it has its own unique policies and birth philosophy. Take the time to learn about your hospital and its views on birth.

Many hospitals offer labor and delivery tours to mothers and their partners. Attend a tour and notice details like how the staff treat fathers, where babies are encouraged to reside after birth, and how mothers are supported during birth. Observing these details will provide you with a number of answers about your hospital's birth philosophy.

Just as important as touring your hospital is talking to your doctor or midwife. You need to be clear on what you can expect the moment you enter the hospital under his or her care. What procedures will the nursing staff want to initiate? What can you opt out of receiving?

As an informed consumer, you should already know your doctor or midwife's cesarean section and epidural rate, even if you anticipate not having one. You should be aware what procedures are common for your practitioner and what you can do to prevent them if you do not want them.

Being an informed consumer means that you place the health and well-being of your baby above any other concerns. When you enter a hospital, you have not given up your right to know about your body and to understand what happens to you. Many hospitals believe this too.

According to the patient's bill of rights adopted by the American Hospital Association (AHA) as early as 1973, "the patient has the right to considerate and respectful care" and "the right to be informed of hospital procedures and practices that relate to patient care, treatment, and responsibilities." The AHA, founded in 1895, is just one of the associations for hospitals that places the rights of the consumer at the heart of their efforts. Mothers who choose hospital births have many advocates that exist to protect them and ensure that they receive quality service.

The Coalition for Improving Maternity Services (CIMS) is made up of individuals and international organizations who are concerned about the care and well-being of mothers, babies, and families. They have devised a rigorous system of designating hospitals, birth centers, and homebirth services as mother friendly. CIMS wants mothers and their families to use this information to evaluate the quality of care in their community. Facilities are also excited about the prospect of declaring to the world that they place mother- and baby-friendly care and services at the heart of their birth philosophies. Currently two birth facilities—one hospital and one birth center—have completed the process and obtained mother-friendly status.

Hospitals, though, are but one of the birth place options a mother has.

BIRTH CENTERS

The National Association of Childbearing Centers (NACC) defines a birth center as

> a homelike facility, existing within a healthcare system with a program of care designed in the wellness model of pregnancy and birth. Birth centers are guided by principles of prevention, sensitivity, safety, appropriate medical intervention, and cost effectiveness. Birth centers provide family centered care for healthy women before, during, and after normal pregnancy, labor, and birth.

NACC, a nonprofit membership organization, was founded over a decade ago. Since then, NACC has been involved in every facet of birth centers; from state regulations and research efforts to national standards and accreditation by the Commission for the Accreditation of Birth Centers. NACC is the premiere organization for birth centers, although a host of state and regional places exist that have worked tirelessly to promote the birth center concept.

This concept has prompted the creation of hundreds of facilities that bring homelike surroundings together with staff and low-level medical equipment for low-risk births. Consumers of birth centers are mothers at low risk for complications who often want more control and fewer interventions during their baby's birth.

Birth centers come in three distinct forms: independent, freestanding facilities that are housed in homelike structures; hospital-linked facilities that are near a maternity department; and facilities that are housed within a hospital yet considered a separate service. Birth centers are usually equipped with private, cozy rooms with queen or full beds, rocking chairs, Jacuzzis, and large kitchens.

Attendants in birth centers are both doctors and midwives who believe that birth is an event that occurs without the need for continuous medical intervention. As an alternative to more technology supported hospital births, birth centers offer a different approach to labor that costs less. Of course, postpartum recovery time in the birth suite is greatly reduced. While a typical hospital stay might last forty-eight to ninety-six hours, discharge from a birth center occurs within six to twelve hours after birth, with additional postpartum visits in the home.

Consequently, the candidates for giving birth in a birth center facility should be mothers who are at low risk for problems during labor and birth, as well as those who will need little to no intervention. Mothers who know in advance that they desire an epidural or other strong pain medication during labor are advised to select another birth site. If these options are chosen during labor at a birth center, transport to a nearby hospital will have to occur. Although this may not be the case in your area, it is typical. All mothers who anticipate a birth center delivery should know what will happen in case a hospital transfer is needed. Discuss this during your prenatal visits with your doctor or midwife.

For many mothers, birth centers represent a welcome change to the technology-driven atmosphere of a hospital. As popular as they have become, birth centers are not the perfect solution for every mother. Some mothers will need more time to adjust to caring for their babies than the short stay that a birth center facility can give them. There are also moms who are not prepared for the level of responsibility that a birth center demands of its clients. Being honest with yourself about these issues will help you decide whether a birth center is the right environment for your baby's birth.

Some moms are denied the option of giving birth in a birth center because their pregnancy is considered high risk. These restrictions, whether coordinated by the birth center or by state regulatory laws, may exclude women from a birth center delivery who actually are low risk for complications during birth. This raises questions about risk factors and the ways practitioners place mothers in a high- or low-risk group. While there is no hard and fast rule about this, it can be a factor in determining your eligibility for this birth site. If you are curious about risk factors in your pregnancy or during birth, talk to your practitioner. Make sure that you ask them how they evaluate certain risks: Is this assessment based on family history, previous birth history, or some other medical model? These are questions about your health and well-being, and you should know the answers.

If you are interested in having your baby at a birth center, you should be aware that many are only open to certain doctors or midwives. This means that your midwife or doctor may not have privileges to bring clients to this facility.

If it is early enough in your pregnancy, you could change practitioners so that you can have your baby in the birth center. However, this is not a decision you should make hastily. You should talk this idea over with your partner and your current practitioner so that you can be certain you are making the best, most informed decision about your baby's birth.

NACC recommends asking a number of questions about any birth center that you are considering. I have modified their list and added to it here.

Questions about birth centers:

✓ Who are the birth attendants in the facility? Doctors? Midwives?

✓ What are their qualifications for working with women in a birth center? Are they licensed or recognized in their state? If not, why?

✓ Is the birth center accredited by the Commission for the Accreditation of Birth Centers?

✓ What are the birth center's procedures for transfer to a hospital?

✓ How much would you have to pay for prenatal care and birth services? What would your insurance company pay?

✓ How soon would you return home after birth?

✓ What follow-up care does the birth center staff offer in the home?

✓ How many births do they have on average each month?

Use this list to put together a profile of the birth centers you are considering. You should feel comfortable with every answer that you are given. NACC recommends that you steer toward nationally accredited birth centers. This accreditation is often in addition to state regulations or licensing. NACC works tirelessly at the national level to create state laws and regulations, yet only thirty-seven states license birth centers or have regulatory laws that apply to their services or facilities. Accreditation is a mark of quality care. Keep this in mind when you contact the birth centers in your area.

I hope that your search will provide you with models like the Women's Wellness and Maternity Center in Madisonville, Tennessee. It is perfectly located to serve two neighboring states as well as large parts of Tennessee.

Staffed by certified nurse midwives, licensed by the state of Tennessee, and accredited by the Commission for the Accreditation of Birth Centers, the Women's Wellness and Maternity Center offers complete maternity care with no regular interventions. The facility has a spacious atmosphere that includes a kitchen, family room, and patio. It even provides a minimum of two home visits by a registered nurse after discharge.

As a further incentive, some birth centers like the one in Tennessee offer gynecological services that include breast exams and pap smears. Many birth centers are becoming much more than places to give birth.

Are all births in a birth center holistic?

Holistic birth is much more than just nice wallpaper and comfortable chairs. It is an approach to birth that integrates mind, body, and spirit.

This type of atmosphere is more likely to exist at a birth center, since its birth philosophy typically considers birth a natural event that should not be medically managed. These facilities believe that support and comfort for the mother is often the key to progressing from contractions to the eventual birth of the baby. The role of every person working in the facility is to help mothers achieve their goal of giving birth.

Nevertheless, for some mothers, this option is not enough. For them, there is simply no place like home.

HOMEBIRTHS

According to the 1999 *National Vital Statistics Report* from the U.S. government, 99 percent of births occurred in a hospital. Of births that occurred outside the hospital, about 65 percent happened in a residence. Birth that occurs in a residence is referred to as a homebirth. Contrary to what you may read, homebirths are not a strange New Age trend.

Births have occurred at home since women began having babies. Today superstars like Cindy Crawford and Pamela Anderson have chosen to have their babies at home. Why? These women and others like them feel that home is the best place to give birth to their babies. Why shouldn't they have their babies in their loving home?

Unfortunately not every mother has a home with a loving environment. Some moms live in unsafe homes with familial conditions that are tenuous, if not downright unpredictable. If this is your situation, your home may not be the best place for your baby to be born. You may want to have your baby there but may need to choose a safer alternative.

There are other issues about homebirths that moms have to ponder. In some places, questions of legality abound. Although it is legal for a mother to have a homebirth, who can attend to her at the birth may present a dilemma.

Doctors are in the minority among practitioners who do homebirths. For a host of political and historical reasons, home care and homebirths changed for doctors over the past decades. Eventually, physician care was offered only at clinics and hospitals. There are still some doctors who make house calls and a few who do homebirths; however, their numbers are dwindling every year.

The practitioners who are the primary attendants at homebirths are midwives. They have been working with women since the beginning of time. How a midwife practices is a matter best left for you to explore in the excellent texts that cover midwifery and women's health. I can tell you that there are states where midwives are scrutinized, supervised, or outlawed from practicing depending on their status as a certified professional midwife, certified nurse midwife, licensed midwife, or direct entry midwife. Each one of these titles denotes a certain type of training and educational background.

Nevertheless, midwives and other homebirth practitioners continue to practice, and come in all shapes, colors, and sizes. Because they are so unique, I have elected not to profile one specific homebirth practice, but rather a homebirth community.

An intentional community was started in Tennessee in the early 1970s by a group of people seeking something more purposeful in their lives. Traveling in caravans throughout the country on a speaking tour, they eventually settled in rural Tennessee where they stayed, had more babies, and grew into a thriving community.

This community needed people to assist mothers giving birth. A group of committed women started supporting mothers, studying birth, working with neighboring doctors, and gathering training year after year. Eventually, a homebirth practice, a midwifery center was born.

It would be easy to reject The Farm and its midwives (who are all still thriving) as a free love–era sideshow, except that these women are talented. Ina May Gaskin, one of the midwives on The Farm, is the president of a national midwifery organization, the Midwives Alliance of North America, and the editor of a birth journal, the *Birth Gazette*. The midwives at The Farm Midwifery Center train doctors from a nearby medical college. And to top it off, their homebirth health outcomes were part of a landmark comparison study with hospital births in the prestigious *American Journal of Public Health*. This study detailed a number of results of care practices, including the fact that The Farm's homebirths included forceps, vacuum extractors, or cesarean sections 2 percent of the time, while the comparative hospital rate for the same procedures was 27 percent. Those are impressive numbers.

The Farm Midwifery Center is but one example of the many practitioners of homebirths who provide maternity care and, in some cases, gynecological care.

If you are considering a homebirth for your baby, here are some questions you need to ask your midwife or doctor, and even more pressing questions for yourself:

✓ Are you prepared to be responsible for your labor and baby's birth?

✓ Do you trust your body's ability to birth your baby?

✓ Would you feel safest during labor and birth within your comfortable home surroundings?

✓ What is your doctor or midwife's philosophy of birth
at home?

Once you have identified your home as your baby's future
birth place, you will need to prepare it for the event. Talk to
your doctor or midwife about any supplies that you should
have on hand—like warm blankets and clean towels. You will
supply all of these items and more. However, don't worry.
Most midwives and doctors give all of their clients a list of
things to have on hand. You will find many of the items at your
local pharmacy or medical supply store, or on-line at homebirth supply companies. There are also mail order companies
that specialize in selling homebirth supply kits. You can find
some of these places listed in the resources section at the end
of this book.

Homebirths, while often very holistic in nature, still need
planning and consideration, just like any other birth. You, as a
mother, still have to consider how to tap into your strength and
energy to give birth.

PLANNING YOUR BABY'S BIRTH
REGARDLESS OF LOCATION

A birth plan is not a list of events that have to occur during a
mother's labor and birth. It is simply a record of the things a
mother and her partner wish their practitioner and birth site
staff would consider doing or avoiding as their baby is born, depending on their situation.

Birth plans typically start first with a mother's birth philosophy before moving on to procedures and policies that are important to her.

Consider your baby's birth for a moment. What type of atmosphere is important to you during his or her arrival? Do you
want it quiet, dark, and intimate? Or would you feel more at

ease with the hustle and bustle of personnel and the judicious use of technology?

Both of these images of birth are only two of the many possibilities that you can choose. Since this book aims to celebrate and embrace pregnancy and birth at a deeper, more intimate level, your choices or plans during your baby's birth can reinforce that.

I have prepared a list of things you may desire for your baby's birth. For your convenience, I have broken the information into three parts: the birth site, labor and birth procedures, and after-birth policies. For now, answer to yourself what is most important to you and skip anything that is immaterial.

The Birth Site

Do you want?

- ❑ The lights on
- ❑ A birthing suite
- ❑ The lights dim
- ❑ A birthing stool
- ❑ A birthing bar
- ❑ A Jacuzzi or tub available
- ❑ Music playing in the room
- ❑ Only required staff in the room or in attendance
- ❑ To labor, birth, and recover in the same room
- ❑ A queen or king sized bed to give birth in

Labor and Birth Procedures

Do you want?

- ❑ To stay home as long as possible before going to the birth site

❏ To go to the birth site immediately when you think you are in labor

❏ To contact your practitioner as soon as you suspect you are in labor

❏ An electronic fetal monitor used constantly to assess the baby's heart rate

❏ An electronic fetal monitor used intermittently to assess the baby's heart rate

❏ A handheld device for checking baby's heart tones

❏ To rupture the amniotic sac during labor

❏ To rupture the amniotic sac only if needed

❏ Medication to deal with pain

❏ No medication to deal with pain

❏ An episiotomy

❏ No episiotomy

❏ An IV

❏ No IV

❏ A labor doula

❏ Your partner with you at all times

❏ Your other children with you during labor

❏ Your other children in another area during labor

❏ Access to food and liquids

❏ Limited access to food and liquid

After-Birth Policies

Do you want?

❏ To breast-feed

❏ Your baby placed on your skin once she is born

❏ Your baby to be placed in your partner's arms after birth

❏ To pull your baby out of your body yourself

❏ Your partner to cut your baby's umbilical cord

❏ Your baby to room-in with you

❏ Your baby to go to the nursery

❏ Your baby to receive eye ointment (a procedure to ward off infection) immediately after birth

❏ To wait until you have greeted your baby before he receives his eye ointment

❏ Your baby to receive any available vaccinations after birth

❏ Your baby not to receive vaccinations after birth

❏ Your baby circumcised

❏ Your baby not to be circumcised

❏ To consult with a lactation consultant soon after birth about breast-feeding

❏ To talk with someone postpartum about baby care

❏ To have a postpartum doula

❏ An early discharge

Once you have picked the items that represent the birth philosophy that you embrace, you need to consider how to create this into a birth plan.

Over the years, birth plans lost their focus and energy, becoming items that were filed away and quickly forgotten by medical staff. The reason? Many were full of accusatory or demanding language, something I do not want your birth plan to have. I want it to be different.

Start by rereading the list you just read. Write down the items that were critically important to you and talk about each item with your doctor or midwife. Get his or her take on all of the things on your list.

Once you have this discussion, you have options about officially composing it.

Some mothers do not feel the need to write down each item into an organized plan. They believe that talking to their practitioner is enough. Other mothers are more concerned with the overall attitude and birth philosophy of their birth site, and consequently want their goals clearly spelled out in a document for all who encounter them during birth.

This document can be a checklist (similar to the one you just read) or a more personal letter. Birth plans can help your birth team know what specific services and labor options you are considering. They are, though, never demands or absolutes. Having a baby is a natural event that can be unpredictable in its magic and its unfolding. Make sure that any birth plan you create states something about unforeseen circumstances, emergencies, and informed consent. With all three of these parts in place, you can guarantee that anyone who reads it will know that you aren't requiring perfection but hoping for a certain amount of consideration and respect for your needs.

To give you some idea of what a birth plan looks like, here is a sample that has me listed as the mother. Try not to copy the words listed here. Instead, read it and hear the language used. Then create one of your own.

As a letter, this incorporates all of the things the fictional pregnant mother has as a birth philosophy. It is inclusive, mentioning the mother's partner and her doula. It also gives an appreciative nod toward the hospital. Notice that words such as "prefer" and "like" are sprinkled throughout the letter. Again, this is because a birth plan is only that, a plan.

SAMPLE BIRTH PLAN

I, Karen Salt, would like to have my baby at Generic Hospital.

Being in such a respected hospital is important to my family during the birth of our first child.

Please be aware that we would like to restrict certain activities to the bare minimum—although we recognize that medical emergencies may change our plans. It is our desire to reach every decision about our baby's birth after careful consideration and discussion. We want to be informed consumers of the hospital.

My support team is David, my husband, and my doula, Kay Smith.

I would like to have limited monitoring during labor with an electronic fetal monitor.

I would also prefer not to have pain medication, since most medication makes me feel sleepy and out of it. I do not want to feel that way during the birth of my baby.

Instead of pain medication, we would like to use the tub and the shower as much as possible and get into a variety of labor-enhancing positions. In order to have continuous movement, I would prefer not to have an IV. I also would prefer not to have an episiotomy during birth.

After our baby is born, one of us would like to be with her at all times. Please advise the postpartum nurse that we would like to room-in with our baby. We are also planning to breast-feed.

Thank you for your efforts to bring our baby into the world.

Signature

You will notice that the mother's practitioner is not mentioned in the sample. Why? Some mothers include the name of their practitioner; others do not. They may feel that their practitioner already knows about their goals since they went over them with him or her. By omitting a name, the mother and her partner may want their goals and desires to be applicable to every doctor or midwife encountered during the birth of their baby.

What you choose to do about your birth plan depends on your own situation. Create one anyway, even if it is just for you. When you are ready to start writing, practice a number of drafts before you settle on one. Once you have your final version, make four copies, giving one to your doctor or midwife, your doula, your birth site, and yourself.

Completing your birth plan helps you to verbalize your birth philosophy. Now you need to consider the actual birth itself. How will you know labor has started? What can you generally anticipate occurring during the many hours it takes a baby to be born?

5

❁ ❁ ❁

LABOR AND BIRTH

I often feel frustrated when I see portrayals of labor on movies
or television shows. Just once, I would like to witness the moment as it could be: A mother, comfortable in her skin, confident in her body, who slowly recognizes the moment for what it
is, the call of birth. Labor is not something to run away from. It
is a connective moment that draws your baby out. With your
body's and your baby's movements, he will venture out of you
and into your lives, ready for the world.

Labor is hard work, but it is hard work spent doing amazing
things. While it took nine long months to grow your baby, it will
take only hours to bring her into the world. She will travel
through sharp and tight spots before nestling in your arms and
eventually capturing your heart.

Of course, you have to get to this moment, and that means
you have to go into labor. Mothers constantly ask me how to
know when labor starts. I truthfully answer that it is hard to not
know that your uterus is constantly contracting and your cervix
is opening. You may not be aware of where you are in the

71

process, but you will know that it is happening. And the more aware you are of your body, the more in tune you will be with many of the subtle changes that herald the onset of labor.

Here are some of the subtle and obvious signs of labor:

You have more than six to eight contractions in an hour. Contractions are intense muscular movements that open your cervix, push your baby into your vagina, and propel her out into the world. What do they feel like? Some moms describe them as menstrual cramps that get progressively more intense as labor continues. They can be felt in a mom's lower back, lower abdomen, and even her upper thighs. As labor continues, you will be able to sense one is coming before it registers on any fetal monitor. Of course, contractions are finicky things that can feel stronger and weaker throughout labor.

Having six to eight contractions is not an immediate indication that you should do anything other than drink some water and put your feet up. Contractions can start due to dehydration or fatigue. If the contractions continue after you have rested and hydrated yourself, you should start to pay attention to them.

Try not to obsess about how frequent they are occurring just yet. The reality is that contracting for an hour does not usually bring about the birth of a baby.

If you are still feeling the sensations after a few hours, tune in to them. Notice how they start and spread across your uterus. Count the interval between each one. You can know how far apart the contractions are by measuring the start of one contraction until the start of another. This means that if a contraction starts at 8:05, and the next one does not start until 8:20, then the contractions are coming every fifteen minutes.

For quite some time, though, contractions may be erratic, coming close together and then moving apart. Again, it is not necessary for you to think too much about them. Instead, notice the patterns that emerge. Do the contractions feel more intense than they did an hour ago? Are they lasting longer? These questions are just as important as the interval between each contraction.

Although labors can be only three hours long, most labors for first-time moms last twelve to fourteen hours. Moms who have already given birth average about seven to eight hours for their second labor. However, these are averages, and your labor may be shorter or longer than these figures.

Your water breaks. Many moms fear that the amniotic sac, which protects their baby in the uterus, will break while they are out shopping. Although this can happen, it is unlikely. Statistics tell us that less than 10 percent of labors start this way. You could be one of them, but the odds are low and I would not fret too much about it. If your amniotic sac ruptures, it will most likely be at night—the time when many labors naturally start.

Breaking the amniotic sac may sound painful, but it is not. The sac is a thin membrane that you cannot feel. Its job is to protect your baby against infections. Throughout pregnancy, until it ruptures in labor or birth, it seals your baby off from the world, keeping her surrounded by amniotic fluid.

Most often, the amniotic sac ruptures on its own during labor without intervention. Once it ruptures, because it is squeezed inside the opening cervix or poked by a baby finger or foot, amniotic fluid leaks out. This fluid will continue to gush or trickle out of the vagina throughout the rest of labor. A mother's body continues to produce amniotic fluid after the amniotic sac has ruptured.

The mucous plug comes out of your cervix. You will remember from your other readings on birth that your mucous plug is the glob of mucous that seals your cervix. It can appear in your underwear (perhaps with a pinkish tinge) once the cervix has opened or dilation has started. It is slightly pink due to the breaking of capillaries when it comes out of the interior of the cervix.

Seeing the mucous plug is a sign that things are happening to your cervix, but not necessarily that your baby is coming immediately. The mucous plug can come out at the beginning of labor or even a week before labor really starts.

I like to think of the mucous plug as a teaser. Its appearance means that things are happening to bring your baby into the world, but not necessarily the main event. More is to come. Patience is the key to seeing the appearance of the mucous plug without feeling the need to prepare birth announcements.

You have a desire to clean your home or cook dinner for six people. This, of course, is the nesting instinct many moms experience during the last days or weeks of pregnancy. Just as a mother bird will arrange and clean her nest for the birth of her young, so too will you. If you are having a hospital birth, then the closest that you will come to nesting is to get your home ready for your postpartum return with your baby. This need to have everything prepared may consume you.

The urge to nest is not as strange as it sounds. It is really just a biological need to prepare your surroundings for your baby. Many moms are not even aware that they are doing it. They only know that something has to be purchased or acquired right now, before their babies are born. Unfortunately, the biological urge meets up with the consumer urge to spend money in order to make a nest ready. Although I do not endorse spending endless sums of money on a baby who simply wants to be fed, clean, and loved, I can understand the drive. Many mothers logically want to have everything ready that their babies might need. Nesting in terms of getting themselves, their partners, or their families ready for a baby can seem foreign.

Yet it is something that you should consider doing. Baby showers, as crazy as they have become, are essentially ways in which a community of women nest for the arrival of a new baby. A newer (some would say older) ritual is a blessing ceremony. During a blessing, the important women in the mother's life gather around her and bless her and her baby, giving both a gift of something that is sacred or important to the giver. The mother's connection to the women who have made the journey to motherhood before her is made clear to her through songs, dances, and poems.

Try a similar sort of shower or blessing with your friends, your partner, and your family. Nest with each group as everyone awaits the arrival of the newest person in your family.

General nesting behavior in a mother is something that a doula can spot a mile away. Mothers who are in nesting mode tend to operate at a hurried, frenzied pace, especially if their consumer urge has met their nesting urge. Sound familiar?

You too may have the sudden desire to bake five trays of lasagna or go to the perfect store miles away for your baby's stroller. If you feel the need to cook everything in your refrigerator and clean every inch of your house, do not let the compulsion override your common sense. The primal impulse you feel is normal and should be embraced; however, this is not the time to operate at marathon speed. Seek help from your family, your partner, and your friends to assist you in readying your home for your baby's arrival.

While you nest, rest and nourish your body for its part in the upcoming birth. Nesting is an opportunity to draw in your swirling thoughts and calm your mind in preparation for birth.

Your baby's head is lying low in your uterus. This interesting sensation is known as engagement. It describes a baby's head that is nestled directly against his mom's cervix. As a clinical definition, this statement omits the fact that it feels as if you have a grapefruit between your legs.

This heavy, low feeling is a good sign that your baby is settling into the pelvic bone structure, readying for birth. It may feel like he is about to fall out, but he's not. All babies need to eventually settle against the cervix. Some little tikes do this weeks before labor starts, while others accomplish it during labor, helping the cervix open through constant pressure from the head.

Engagement has another benefit. After spending weeks feeling as if your lungs were being pushed out the top of your body by your growing uterus, you will finally be able to breathe more easily once your baby moves down. When this happens, some mothers might tell you that it looks like your baby has dropped. He has.

You have a knowing feeling that something is different. You have an inner radar that tells you many things. Some women refer to this gift as intuition or listening to their sixth sense. When it comes to mothers and their children, I believe that this intuitive knowledge is very much alive. You are able to sense when things feel different and often know that some "change" is coming. In your case, this change is birth.

You may wake up one morning in your last weeks of pregnancy and know that your body is ready to give birth. Without any immediate conscious knowledge, you are registering on a subconscious level the many changes occurring inside your body. It is as if your baby is whispering that it is time for her to come out.

Doulas listen to a mother's intuition. Often considered less credible than technological assurances, a mother's intuition is steeped in knowledge that spans the beginning of humanity. Countless women have listened to their intuition suggest that they take a certain fork in the road of life or check on their children.

A few years back, best-seller lists and talk shows were full of people talking about the power of intuition. Although they may have dropped off the radar, the notion of intuition has not. It still drives endless romantic movies, soap opera plots, career decisions, and, yes, even authors like me to try new things and listen to the wisdom of the ages that has kept many a mother and her child safe.

Listen to your intuition when it announces your baby's imminent arrival.

You experience bowel/stomach imbalances. Both of these problems can result from a virus or some other cause. However, experiencing them without any other symptoms of being sick is often a good indication that contractions are happening. Why? Your uterus contracts frequently throughout your pregnancy. You are probably noticing them more if you are seven or eight months pregnant. These tightenings get progressively stronger and more intense as labor nears.

Of course, the rhythmic tightenings of the uterus can irritate the parts of the body that are squished by it, notably, the intestines and the stomach. Even before you register the contractions of the uterus, your body responds to this irritation, often by giving you diarrhea or nausea.

It may seem odd, but this natural cleansing is helpful. It allows the body to go into labor without heavy, undigested food (like lasagna), gas, or other matter pressing against the uterus.

If you experience vomiting or diarrhea, notify your practitioner. He or she would want to rule out any other concern. As a precaution, drink plenty of water and stay near a bathroom until the feeling passes.

You find yourself focusing within yourself. Some mothers start to remove themselves from the boisterousness of life in the days before labor starts. It's almost as if they do not want anything else to intrude on their babies' time.

Mothers who are still actively working or socializing may feel "zoned out" when they start to "zone in" to their babies. Tasks become harder to focus on and conversations become jumbled. In essence, the mental, physical, and spiritual energy it takes to get ready for birth distracts them from life.

Granted, this distraction could easily be due to general pregnancy fatigue. However, it is often more than just that. To participate in labor is a draining, albeit revitalizing experience. Your body knows this and decides to help you lessen the load, so to speak. Your brain sends signals that the things happening outside your body are not as important as the things occurring inside.

If you find yourself counting change four times at the store during the last weeks of your pregnancy and forgetting to do simple chores, take a minute to quiet your mind and listen. You may be receiving signals from your body about your baby's birth that you are ignoring.

Many of my doula signs address the earliest moments of labor. Early labor is a time of adjustment. Active labor needs no introductions or signs to herald its occurrence. That's because active labor is intense and eventful, as well as intimate and quiet.

Labor and birth occur for each mother in a way that is particular to her body, her baby, and her circumstances. As long as there is no medical reason why labor should not start on its own, a mother will experience one of the ways labor can begin mentioned earlier in this chapter. Once it begins, it evolves at its own pace, depending on variables such as positions used to advance labor, use of pain medication, and even maternal fatigue.

Your labor could follow the average of twelve to fourteen hours for a first birth, or close to seven for mothers who have previously given birth. It could also be very short or very long.

Short labors last less than four hours from beginning to end and feel like a fast-moving train has taken over the body. Moms who have a history of quick labors should pay close attention to their bodies during the last weeks of pregnancy so that they can interpret even the slightest changes. If this is something that you can anticipate, talk to your practitioner and prepare for a potentially quick labor. He or she might suggest changing or adjusting plans accordingly. One typical change you could anticipate with a history of short labors is leaving home for the birth site soon after the onset of contractions.

Mothers who experience prolonged labors face the opposite task. They need their strength and courage to continue laboring while progress remains slow. Just as in the parable of the tortoise and the hare, it matters not how quickly you finish the race but believing that you can do it, even if it takes you longer than someone else. If you already have a history of long labors, spend some time talking with your practitioner about ways that you can work with your body to help labor progress at its own pace. This may not make labor go any faster, but at least you will have a list of coping strategies that can make the experience more comfortable.

Whether long or short, your labor will bring your baby into the world.

For specific possibilities, read the following labor patterns observed by professionals at countless other births.

FIRST STAGE OF LABOR

Labor is composed of three distinct stages. The first stage is notable because it includes all of the efforts of a mother's body to open the cervix and move it to its full opened size of about ten centimeters in diameter. Of course, it can take hours for the cervix, which pokes into the top of the vagina, to thin in thickness and open. Both the acts of thinning and opening take hours to complete. Luckily, it often occurs at the same time. The cervix thins in a manner similar to pulling a thick rubber band between one's fingers. As the contractions of the uterus tighten rhythmically, the cervix slowly opens. Your cervix may or may not be thinning or opening at the start of your first stage of labor.

Early Labor

The first stage of labor is composed of various parts. The initial part of the first stage of labor is referred to as early labor. Things are happening during early labor, but in an inconsistent way. Contractions start and last for hours but they can stop for no apparent reason. Some moms feel pressure in their lower back or deep within their pelvis.

All of these sensations are indications that early labor may be occurring. Do not rush about planning for your baby's imminent birth, though, if you feel any of them. Early labor can last for days. Because a mother may not be fully aware that she is in early labor, she's often surprised at one of her last prenatal visits to hear that her cervix is already two or three centimeters dilated.

Some mothers consider this imperceptible dilation a sign that all of labor will occur this quietly. By the time these mothers reach four to five centimeters in dilation, they clearly understand why early labor is not called active labor. Active labor needs no introduction.

While you are still experiencing early labor, what can you, your partner, or even your doula do to calm you down and strengthen you up?

Things You Can Do for Yourself. Early labor is usually a quiet time that can set your adrenaline going. Intent on counting contractions, excited about the prospect of having your baby, and anxious about what may lie ahead, you may invest an incredible amount of energy in wishing labor along when you should be relaxing, eating, or resting.

The temptation to daydream about your baby is so bewitching that sleep and even food become an afterthought. This is the time to channel all of your energy on being ready for birth.

Take in light foods like soup, bread, and fruit. Keep it simple. Your stomach has tossed in the towel on digesting large quantities of food. Why? Most of the blood in your body is going to support your vital organs and your uterus. This supplies your baby with oxygen-rich blood. Unfortunately, your stomach is not high on your body's list of vital areas.

You also have to deal with a much slower digestive system. Help your body by ingesting simple foods that are rich in vitamins and minerals, full of energy-enhancing agents, and easy to digest.

But food isn't the only thing you need. Your body will go through an amazing event during labor. And no matter how it occurs, your body will need to be well rested. Like a marathon runner, you wouldn't dream of starting a race without any sleep. I know, I know. You are many months pregnant and sleep is a luxury you haven't had. Humor me. Try to get some sleep. Put your feet up. Stack pillows against the headboard of your bed and breathe deeply. Even if you are too jazzed to sleep during early labor, try to turn off your mind for a few minutes.

Vary your positions. Sit in a chair. Lie down. Walk. Stand. It may take hours before your cervix reaches three to four centimeters in dilation. Starting active labor fatigued will not help your body through each contraction.

Having said this, I understand that you will need to do something or go crazy. Here are some things that you can do during early labor, other than rest:

Call your practitioner. Let your doctor or midwife know that you think you are in labor and ask what your next course of action should be. This will probably depend on your labor signs and any other protocols that they need to follow.

Call your doula. If you have chosen to have a labor doula, contact her and let her know that things are happening. She'll let you know when to expect her.

Recheck your labor bag. Make sure that your bag contains all of the comfort aids that you will need throughout labor, and all of the supplies you and your baby will need after birth. Don't forget to have a few things for your partner—including food.

81

Practice comfort measures. You considered a number of re-laxation techniques during pregnancy. Practice them now during early labor with each contraction to see whether or not you feel comforted.

The most important thing to do is to listen to your body. Hydrate it. Rest it. Feed it. And pay attention to the way you interpret the contractions. Your emotions play a major part in how you imagine your labor feels.

Things Your Partner Can Do. Your partner's role is critical during early labor. As the watcher, not the one experiencing labor, he or she is able to help you by tending to the other concerns in your life that need managing before a doula or practitioner comes into the picture.

Here is a quick list of some of the essential things a partner can do during this time:

1. Pack a labor bag if one is not complete.

2. Tend to any children who may be preparing to go with an attendant or helper during labor.

3. Prepare food and drinks for the time at home and during labor at the birth site.

4. Observe the intensity and frequency of the contractions.

5. Call the doula or the practitioner for you so that you can focus on relaxing.

6. Prepare the home for labor. Pull out pillows, clean towels, waterproof pads, and other supplies purchased at a medical supply shop or pharmacy. Your

doula can provide you with a list of things that you might want to have on hand.

7. Check to make sure that the telephone numbers of all the people to call after birth are in the labor bag.

8. Work with you to relax and release tension. Encourage you to rest and eat lightly.

ESSENTIAL THINGS TO HAVE DURING LABOR
1. Food for you and your partner
2. Clothes for you during labor and postpartum
3. Slippers
4. Socks
5. Toothbrush and toothpaste
6. A bathrobe
7. Lip balm
8. Hair essentials: clips, headbands, scrunchies
9. Shampoo: travel size
10. Moisturizer or lotion: travel size, unscented
11. Camera/video camera loaded with film, cassette, or disc
12. Clothes for baby after birth, such as a sleeper or newborn gown with socks or booties, a blanket, and a cap. If the weather is cold, include mittens and a snowsuit for travel back home
13. Diapers: at least enough for the ride home from the hospital or birth center

---

Things Your Doula Can Do. If you hire a doula for your labor and birth, she will most likely not be with you when you have your first contraction or other first sign of labor. Never fear. You will simply call her when you feel her presence is required.

One of the best things about choosing a doula is that she is available for the mother; either in person or by telephone. Let your doula know what you are feeling during early labor. She may be able to calm anxieties or help lessen lingering tension. She may come to you or wait to come later.

The most important thing she can do for you during early labor is offer emotional and physical support. Gentle words of encouragement can go a long way to help a mother believe that she's not alone in experiencing one of the most transforming events in her life.

Active Labor

Active labor is the middle part of the first stage of labor. During this time, the cervix stretches from four to eight centimeters in dilation. Contractions typically pick up in strength, becoming increasingly regular and frequent. During active labor, the rhythmic tightenings of the uterus are often two to five minutes apart and last about forty to sixty seconds.

They might not last long, but contractions cause immense change to the cervix. A contraction is effective because the bands of muscles at the upper part of the uterus tighten, causing the lower part of the uterus, the cervix, to slowly open. The cervix is pulled up with each contraction.

A secondary action is also occurring with each contraction. The pressure from the contraction forces the baby against the cervix and further down into the pelvis.

By the end of active labor, contractions come quickly. Mothers also tend to tune in internally. Everything recedes during active labor. Noises, voices, even people move out of the consciousness of a laboring mother as she focuses her energy on navigating the waves of tightenings that crest and rise throughout her body.

Things You Can Do for Yourself. This part of labor is active for a reason. The contractions are more potent and require a variety of strategies to move from one to the next.

Although you may experience a short, then a long, then another short contraction, a pattern will eventually emerge. As labor continues and your cervix opens, your entire body will be involved in each contraction. To minimize your discomfort, assume a variety of positions that will encourage your baby to drop into your pelvis. This will help open your cervix more with each contraction.

As you focus on a contraction, let yourself greet each one as it appears by taking in a deep breath and then maintaining a natural in-and-out rhythm. Breathe slowly as long as it feels comfortable. Try not to take in and exhale air in a quick, jerky manner. It is easy to hyperventilate like this. Remember that the air you bring into your body travels as oxygen-filled blood to your baby. If you hold your breath, you will rob your baby of oxygen, something that can potentially cause her damage.

The best way to center on your contractions is to seek ways to exist with them, to view them as essential components for the birth of your baby. When you exist with them, labor becomes something to experience rather than something to endure. Am I suggesting that labor is easy? I'm not. There is probably nothing as demanding and challenging as giving birth to a baby. It is likely the hardest work you will ever do. Yet it is possible, regardless of whether you choose pain medication or not, to work with labor rather than against it.

To work with your contractions during active labor, try a variety of comfort aids like water, light touch, massage, scents, or heat. These aids will help you focus more on your contractions and less on other outside things.

There is one other thing that you can do for yourself to help your labor progress. Try not to look at the clock. In fact, I would suggest that you remove all clocks from your line of vision. Time means nothing to a laboring mom. Your only marker of your labor is your body's responses to the contractions and your baby's progress into the pelvis region.

By constantly checking the clock (and the temptation to do so is overwhelming), you make the hours of labor become more important than the baby inside you. Unless there is a medical reason why anyone should focus on the time it takes you to move from one number to the next in cervical dilation, ignore time. Your labor will happen at its own pace.

LABOR WARNING SIGNS:
CALL YOUR DOCTOR OR MIDWIFE IF YOU HAVE:
1. Any sharp or sudden pain in your abdomen
2. Cramps in your abdomen or uterus area
3. Bleeding from your vagina that appears bright red
4. Fluid from your vagina that is not clear—more like green or light green
5. Fluid from your vagina that smells foul
6. Headaches, dizziness, or blurred vision

Things Your Partner Can Do. Many partners become exhausted during active labor as they work off adrenaline, lose sleep, or suffer from nerves. To keep your partner rested and ready to help you, talk to him now about ways to keep his stamina up. Make sure he eats, drinks, and rests in preparation for the birth right along with you during the last days or weeks before birth and especially during active labor.

A QUICK NOTE TO YOUR LABOR PARTNER
Comforting a mom during labor and birth is not easy. Contrary to the ways TV shows and movies present birth, your partner will not yell at you, call you names, or pull your lower lip over your face. (Thank you, Bill Cosby.)

What she will do is be in labor with you by her side. She will be amazing, fascinating, beautiful, and uncomfortable at times.

To relieve her discomfort and uncertainty:

Just be there.   You cannot have the baby for her, but you can let her know that you are there for her.

Learn techniques that can help her.   Do not pretend to be superhuman. You are not and she knows it. Instead of pretending that you know everything, learn specific techniques. This section lists many that you can add to your labor comfort list.

Do not pretend that you understand what she is going through.   Unless you have had a baby, she will not be impressed.

If you have hired a doula, work with her as a team.   Your partner's doula is not there to do anything better than you. She cannot take your place, and she doesn't want to. You are the partner that the mother needs.

One of the most important things your partner can do during this time is remember the various labor positions learned in childbirth class. Your doula can suggest them during active labor, but you and your partner should already know what feels good to your nonlaboring body. For example, if you have weak knees, you should avoid any squatting positions unless people on either side are holding you up. Hands-and-knees positions are also out unless you have pillows cushioning your joints.

Here is a list of positions for active labor that you and your partner can try now. Different positions have different benefits. Some open up the pelvic bone structure—achieved during squatting—so that baby can settle more easily into that space. Other positions, like walking, use gravity to encourage a baby to settle against the cervix. Choose the positions during active labor that will help your labor progress.

Positions for Active Labor

Walking.   This is a natural labor enhancer. Walking stimulates blood flow and moves the baby against the cervix. When you go walking, make sure that your partner or your doula takes some clean obstetrical pads and towels along just in case you leak amniotic fluid during contractions.

Rocking Hips from Side to Side and Front to Back. This feels wonderful. You can do it while leaning against the counter, kneeling on your bed, or standing in your partner's arms. It really helps to settle baby's head into the pelvic area. Rocking the hips can also help rotate a stubborn baby from lying with the back of its head against its mother's back to the more comfortable position of the back of its head against its mother's front.

Leaning on or against something. You can lean against your partner, your doula, your bed, a building, or even a tree. You can face any direction you choose. The goal is to give your weight over to something or someone else.

Straddling a Chair. This opens your pelvic area and gives your legs some rest. Pick a comfortable chair that has a backrest. Place a couple of pillows against the back to make sitting with your round belly more comfortable. Lean into the pillows during each contraction. The chair should have a large sitting area so that you can sit and fit your belly against the back without having to hunch your back into a curve.

Squatting. You can get into a squat either by being supported by your partner or doula behind you, holding you up, or by grabbing on to the seat of a chair or sofa yourself. If you are squatting with someone behind you, squat between their legs and place your elbows on their thighs and your hands on their knees. Lean back against them. Try to give them your weight. If you are squatting while holding on to a chair or a sofa, try to use the object to help hold you up. If you have weak knees or legs, do not choose this position. It requires you to keep your knees bent at a sharp angle.

Kneeling on All Fours. This position can help relieve the pressure of a quick moving labor or relieve the strain of back labor. If kneeling on all fours hurts your knees, place pillows under your knees to cushion the impact on your joints. Rocking your hips from side to side in this position or having someone massage your lower back can help relieve sharp discomfort caused by a rotating baby's head.

Lying Down. This position entails lying on your side (choose your left to increase blood circulation) with pillows between your knees, under your belly, and against your head and back. Use this position to catch a few minutes of sleep between contractions, or to conserve your energy before getting into another position or taking a walk. Be warned: If contractions have become irregular, your practitioner will want you to move.

Use Your Imagination. The truth is that you can benefit from any position that comforts you and helps labor progress. Use your imagination to come up with various positions that feel good to you.

Helping you into positions is just one way that your partner can help you face your contractions and exist with them. He or she can utilize many other comforting techniques.

LABOR COMFORTS

Touch A-Z

Massage is something that feels good after a long day at work and can feel heavenly during active labor. In Part 1, I talked about the benefits of massage during pregnancy. The same benefits extend to labor.

Mothers who are riding the waves of tightenings may clench their other muscles during the peak of the contractions. This constant clenching and unclenching makes a mother even tenser as she fights her body's added stress. It is thought by birth professionals that the less relaxed a mother is, the less effective her contractions will be on her cervix.

How can you eliminate tension? Your partner (or your doula) can stroke your body and remind you to release your muscles during each contraction. At this time, you probably only want a light touch.

Toward the end of active labor, light touch is no longer enough. This may be the time that you need a heightened connection to the people around you. Some moms achieve this without someone touching them at all. They get a sense of connection by having someone near them, practically inches from their face, breathing words of encouragement. Knowing that someone else is there can help a mom find the strength to embrace all that labor has to give. It may sound hokey, but it is true. One of the earliest research studies on doulas found that a mother responded positively to the presence of another woman in the room with her during labor, even if that woman didn't say anything to her.

There are moms, though, who desire the collective energy of every hand in the birthing room, guiding them through active labor. Someone who peeked in the birthing room during a contraction would see a scene that looked like a rendering of some ancient, intricate puzzle, as both doula and partner connect themselves to the mother through their hands.

As active labor progresses, massage that is more specific may be required. Mothers who experience pressure in their lower back may need a sacrum rub. Your partner can find your sacrum by working up from your tailbone and locating the bony area at the base of your spine that is about the size of the palm of an adult hand. The sacrum is a group of connected bones that fan out like butterfly wings. This bone structure is at the back of your pelvic area.

Your baby's head has to move past your sacrum to get into the birth canal. The sacrum, made more flexible by hormones, actually spreads apart a bit to let baby's head go by. During labor, this can feel like a small rock is pressing against your lower back.

A sacrum rub can alleviate any strain and pressure, at least temporarily. Have your partner or your doula press the flat part of the palm of either hand against the sacrum. This motion applies counterpressure to the pressure exerted by the baby's head. Counterpressure can also be applied to the sacrum by rubbing a tennis ball back and forth over it or by using a massage tool designed for the back called a spinal roll.

The sacrum is only one part of the body that can benefit from counterpressure and deep massage. Talk to your partner about other places that you would like to have touched during labor.

MAKING YOUR OWN HOT COMPRESSES

Many hot compresses are activated packs that require the user to squeeze or open a pouch that is floating inside chemicals in the pack. Once the contents of the pouch mix with the chemicals in the pack, a reaction takes place that releases heat. This heat makes the entire pack hot, until the reaction is complete.

These types of hot packs are one-time use items. They are thrown away after they are used. When a mother is in labor, she does not want to worry about having to pop and shake something in order to get relief.

There is an alternative. You can create your own hot compresses. Homespun hot compresses can be beautiful, square shaped creations in muslin cloth that even come with fabric covering. (I own three different sizes of these.)

However, hot compresses do not have to be so elaborate. You can create your own using things you already have in your home.

Needed
1 measuring jug or cup
1 full calf-length sock with no holes
1 to 2 cups of uncooked rice, depending on length of sock
fr 1/4 to 1/2 cup of dried herbs (choose something like lavender)
1 bobbin of cotton thread
1 sewing needle
1 mixing bowl

After you have gathered all of your supplies, place the rice and herbs into the mixing bowl. Mix evenly to help disperse the herbs throughout the rice. Next, pour the rice-herb mixture into the sock. Once you have completed that task, stitch the top of the sock closed. You can do a "blanket stitch," the stitches that you see on the edge of blankets, to bind the sock tight.

You can also fold the top of the sock over and perform a "running stitch." Running stitches run from right to left with small gaps between each stitch. If you would like a tighter seal, do another running stitch in a line underneath the first one.

Test your finished hot compress by placing it in the microwave for about a minute. Check the temperature with the front or back of your hand. If it is too hot, wrap the compress in a towel. This displaces the heat so that it has to travel through the towel before arriving at your skin. (A good doula tip to use during labor.) If it is not hot enough, warm it up again for an additional minute.

Your doula and your partner can use this hot pack during labor, applying it to tense or throbbing muscles or joints. It is quickly warmed and reusable.

Water

Many moms report a lessening of the intensity of contractions standing under the shower or soaking in the tub. Bunched muscles relax. Tension often releases. There is also another potential benefit. When moms feel tranquil and calm, as they typically do in water, active labor goes faster.

If you would like to use water during your labor, consider your options. Standard bathtubs, like the one you have in your home, are usable. Just make sure that the tub is clean and you can soak comfortably while sitting. You can roll towels or purchase bath pillows to place behind your neck. Because most home bathtubs are small, you will not be able to stretch fully or get into a variety of positions. Some hospitals have responded to this need by installing large tubs in labor rooms to accommodate a pregnant mother in a variety of poses.

In a standard tub, keeping the water at body temperature is a frustrating act of heating then cooling and heating again. It might be challenging, but it is essential. Setting the tub at the body's base temperature is safe and comforting to the skin. Any temperature higher than that and a mother may feel overheated.

One alternative to dealing with tubs is to stand or sit in the shower. Showers give the same benefits of water as tubs, but with two important differences: Being in the shower too early does not adversely affect contractions, and no one has to deal with the hassle of maintaining temperate water. Another plus is that many shower heads are adjustable and can be pulled down and directed at one particular area of the body. Unlike the bath, though, the entire body is not surrounded by water and can become chilled. Standing can also become tiresome between and during powerful contractions. Fortunately, both of these challenges are surmountable.

You can maintain your retention of heat in the shower by using this doula tip. Have your partner (or your doula) place towels around your neck, shoulders, and back. Advise him to keep the towels constantly wet. I have used this tip often during labors. Mom stays warm from the heated water on the towels, and the towels help hold in her body heat, reducing chilled skin. This simple solution gives the impression of the enveloping warmth of the tub without actually being in it.

Now, the other challenge, a mom tiring while standing, is also easily overcome by planning. Long showers are now possible by sitting mom in a water-tolerant chair. One option is to pick up a large plastic chair that has slip-proof pads on the bottom, a backrest, and a wide seat. Cover the seat with towels and you could probably stay in that position for hours.

Another option is to bring a small stool into the shower. The only problem with stools is that many are made of wood and will not survive being in the water. You will also find that many of the inexpensive stools come without backs, making them uncomfortable for long sitting. Of course, you can always abandon using any sitting apparatus and opt instead for the solid form of your partner. Have him or her come into the shower and be your chair during active labor.

The final water option for active labor that we will discuss is neither the bathtub nor the shower. It is a small birthing pool. Birthing pools are circular plastic spas that allow a mom to lean against the sides and immerse herself up to her breasts in water. Some pools are big enough for two people; others are big enough for just mom.

Laboring in pools is something that is decades old. (Some even say that it has even older origins, dating to the distant past.) A doctor named Michel Odent was one of the first Western practitioners to set up birthing pools in all of his laboring rooms for his clients. He advocated the use of water during labor because he believed that women have natural endorphins—pain-reducing chemicals that we all make—that can surge during labor as long as moms are not threatened and are able to labor undisturbed in a quiet atmosphere. Odent felt that in this birth atmosphere a woman could give birth without drugs or intervention, relying only on her body.

The laboring mother of today may choose to use a birthing pool because of Odent's example. However, she could opt for one simply because she likes the way water makes her feel. Many women add water to their labor comforts because it helps them relieve tension in their bodies during labor. This isn't a guarantee. Studies have shown that immersing in water before active labor starts can actually slow or stop contractions.

Today, hospitals, birth centers, and homes have Jacuzzis, large tubs, and birthing pools for laboring moms. There are also a number of places that are receptive to moms bringing their own portable units with them. Portable tubs or pools are easy and quick to install. They often come with a converter to fill from the tap, a disposable liner that goes inside the pool, a heater to keep the water at body temperature, and a thermometer. What's really nice about this setup is that you can obtain a rental unit that is shipped to you weeks before labor starts. You simply drain, rinse, and ship it back to the provider sometime after the birth. This type of service sounds like it should cost thousands of dollars, but the actual cost is a fraction of that.

Birthing pool rental kits from the Global Maternal/Child Health Association, one of the premier waterbirth organizations, cost about $250 as of press time. This fee includes everything a person needs for a birthing pool, including a liner, a dual heater system, drain pump, and faucet adapter. This same group provides pools for purchase that also come with every item needed for use. They were priced at press time at $995.

If you are interested in laboring in water, check your options carefully at home and at your birth site. As you can see from this discussion, it is possible to use water any way that you like. Before you decide on anything, you should have the support of your doctor or midwife. Most practitioners have seen the benefits of using water during labor.

Body Fuel

Most moms imagine laboring with soft lights, gentle music, warm water, and no food. This combination will ensure one thing: that a mother will not have enough strength to make it to the end of labor. Without fuel, your muscles work harder than they need to, making contractions hurt more with little cervical progress.

Hospitals used to have a policy that required mothers to abstain from food during labor. The only substances they were allowed to chew on or suck were ice cubes and wet towels. Yuck. This policy was in place in hospitals where many laboring mothers were given general anesthesia. Although this is not the case now, there are some hospitals that still enforce this no-food rule.

For you, the big question is not, Will you be able to eat? but, What should you choose? As your cervix dilates beyond five centimeters, you will not want to eat much of anything. It is almost as if your stomach sends a signal to your brain that says "no more food please." Instead of food, you may only want drinks. Diluted, unsweetened fruit drinks and mineral water are excellent choices.

Many moms suck on hard candy for some instant sugar or nibble on frozen fruit pops. Dried fruits are also a good idea. Some enterprising mothers prepare or obtain electrolyte replacement drinks that can give them the right balance of sugar and salts that their bodies need during labor. One of these options may be just what you need. Yet you aren't the only one who needs nourishment.

While it's important that you provide fuel for your body, your partner also needs food. Make sure that he brings items for himself. Do not let him leave your side to go to the cafeteria, as I see many fathers doing. Pack a cooler with things for both of you. Put in wipes (unscented) for napkins and long straws. Why the straws? You will not have the strength to open your mouth as you near transition.

DEHYDRATION

It is easy to get dehydrated during labor. Some moms think that they are drinking enough, only to find that labor is slowing and they feel weak. A simple blood test often shows signs of dehydration. To prevent this problem, many practitioners want mothers to receive an IV immediately upon admission to the hospital. Practitioners who work at homebirths or in birth centers typically do not use IVs. They prefer to have mothers hydrate themselves.

To hydrate yourself, take a long sip of a drink after each contraction. This will have you drinking every couple of minutes by the time you reach transition.

By eating and drinking, at least initially, when your body tells you to, you are giving your uterus the best chance of being as strong as possible.

Yet fuel is only part of claiming your strength during active labor. You also need to use your senses to move through each contraction.

Visualization and Imagery

It can be hard to relax during active labor when you are grappling with something so challenging. Although it may be easy to dwell on the challenges of labor, I want you to focus on your baby. See her little body with each contraction. Imagine her tiny fingers opening and closing. Watch her mouth open for her thumb. Every time she moves during a contraction, comfort her. Talk to her and rub your belly. Tell her that everything is all right and that she will be out soon. Do this with your partner.

And during active labor think of your body too. Try to see your cervix opening like a flower. The puckered lips at the end of your cervix actually open like a rose to allow your baby into your birth canal. See yourself opening more with each contraction.

As intense as the contractions may be, every single one serves a purpose. Each one brings your baby closer to you.

I also want you to acknowledge that this time in labor may be painful. Many women experience some form of discomfort or pain during labor. However, each mother registers that pain within her threshold of pain that is unique to her. What one mom might consider unbearable, another might not notice. We will discuss more about pain later in this section during a discussion of pain medication.

Regardless of the discomfort or pain that you may perceive during labor, you have to visualize birth as something powerful, something important. No matter what arises during labor or how your birth turns out, it is a life-changing event for your entire family.

SOUNDS

Playing music during active labor can have a hypnotic effect, taking you to the comforting parts of yourself and allowing you to calm your nerves. It can also help bring a familiar item from your home or life into an unfamiliar setting, such as a hospital labor room. Have your partner prepare a CD or tape of your favorite music. Remember to pack it in your labor bag.

As beneficial as sound is, it does not have to come from outside you. Many moms moan or almost sing during labor as a basic response to the contractions of the uterus and the opening of the cervix. If you want to make noise, go for it. Watch for any tension in the neck and throat. Some doulas recommend mothers strive for a low, more relaxed sound when moaning versus a higher pitch.

Things Your Doula Can Do.   Doulas are usually with a mother during active labor. As you know, active labor is often the time that mothers need immense physical and emotional support.

Your doula will probably be busy creating a pleasing atmosphere for you by keeping you comfortable. She may provide warm towels or blankets, give massages—especially lower back massages, get you into a variety of labor-enhancing positions, and inform you of certain procedures or techniques, if you have questions that your doctor or midwife has not answered.

Your doula, though, is more than just a fount of wisdom; she is first and foremost a champion of mothers, babies, and families—no matter their makeup and design. This means that she isn't pushing for some type of birth outcome or striving for you to have your baby a certain way. If during active labor you choose something that you previously felt you didn't want, such as pain medication, your doula will remind you of your decision, ask you to wait about five minutes to see if you still feel the same way, and then back whatever choice you make.

Doulas also bring with them something I have heard referred to as a magical bag—a large canvas bag stuffed with hot packs, birth balls, massage oil, and other doula invented and tested tools that could potentially aid a mother during her labor and baby's birth. My bag contains hot packs of various sizes, breast creams for split nipples, large waterproof pads to place under mom, forms to fill out, a stethoscope, a doll-sized baby with placenta and pelvis, latex gloves, massage oil, and handouts of community services. I might add or remove certain items depending on the needs of the family. Talk to your doula about what's in her doula bag.

TRANSITION

Transition is actually the last part of the first stage of labor. During this time, a mother's body transitions between actively relaxing and embracing each contraction to physically meeting them head on while pushing. The contractions often come one to three minutes apart and last about a minute and a half in duration.

Some mothers experience transitions that last for three contractions. Another mother may have an hour of intense pressure and occasional urges to push as her cervix moves from eight centimeters to full dilation.

The baby is now deep in the pelvis; its head is heavy against the cervix, causing incredible amounts of pressure throughout the perineum.

The primal need to push against this pressure heralds the second stage of labor. Pushing should only occur if it is safe for the baby to enter the birth canal. Your practitioner will encourage you when it is time.

Although the desire to push can appear during transition, many moms experience a lull in contractions once they reach full dilation. I think this happens because a mother's body knows that it needs to switch gears from relaxing alongside contractions to pushing with them. When the contractions in her body cease for a moment, a mom is able to regroup and get her bearings for the next stage of labor.

Some mothers want to share the birth of their new baby with their other children. If you want your children to be present, you need to do a few things now in preparation.

1. Talk to each one about the reality of blood, noise, and pain during labor and birth. As much as you may want them with you, it is important that they recognize that birth is a physically demanding event. You can help them learn about the beauty and the challenges of labor by showing them videos and letting them take a tour of your birth site. Some places even have a class for children who want to be present during birth. Make sure that they know that the decision to be there is one that you will let them decide on their own.

2. Talk to them about how you might look and sound during labor. They should be prepared for that. Let them know that if they are uncomfortable at any time during labor, they can leave the birth room.

3. Younger children, often those under five or even older, if sensitive, may have a hard time being sepa-

rated from you or your partner for the birth. Enlist the help of a support person who is there just for them. Try to choose someone they love to be with versus someone they do not know well.

Things You Can Do for Yourself. Transition often feels like labor will never end. It will. During transition, repeat a mantra to yourself: One contraction at a time. Remembering this sound advice will help you see the benefit and the need of every contraction that graces your body. Each one helps your cervix reach full dilation.

Do something else during this time: Keep your team beside you. Even if you aren't sure what your doula, your partner, or your practitioner can do for you, don't let them out of your sight. Their presence might be just what you need to move to full dilation and get ready for pushing.

Things Your Partner Can Do. Partners are quite shell-shocked during transition. Many do not believe that labor is actually nearing an end, especially if the contractions kick up in strength. Don't worry if your partner becomes dazed. Labor is often a long and powerful act for partners. It can be frustrating for him to watch you bear all the discomfort of labor without taking away any of the pain.

Although your partner may be unsure what to do, he has to remember that he is your anchor. His touch and encouragement can aid you to the next stage.

Talk to him now about the various stages of birth so that transition becomes something that both of you can anticipate and prepare for.

Things Your Doula Can Do. If you have a labor doula with you, she will watch carefully for signs of what will help you to the next stage of birth. Often she will establish a pattern for you of sipping water, breathing, moaning, and massaging to get you through the contractions of transition. Hot packs may be in constant motion on your back. In addition, a doula may even arrange her body in a variety of poses in order to support a mother in the positions of her choice. A doula's role during transition is to provide whatever support she can so that a mother can prepare to push her baby out into the world.

SECOND STAGE OF LABOR

Pushing

Pushing tends to require internal concentration as a mother releases her perineal muscles in a manner similar to having a bowel movement. The band of muscles that encircle all your female genitalia are involved in this action.

There are toning exercises that you can do now to increase your recognition of and use of your perineal muscles. Talk to your doula or your practitioner about Kegel exercises. As beneficial as these exercises are, pushing during birth is a physical act that is best learned on the job.

It can take anywhere from fifteen to twenty minutes to nearly three hours to move your baby through your vagina and out into the world. This procedure would be simple if babies did not have to turn, maneuver their heads, and lower their bodies between and through their mothers' pelvic bones.

There is a pelvic bone, the symphysis pubis, that connects the two sides of the pelvis. You can feel it by touching the bone that is hidden in your pubic hair just below your abdomen. Your baby has to turn to move the largest part of his or her head under this bone before rotating again to get his or her shoulders born. This rotating and turning can take some time to accomplish, especially for larger babies.

By the time a baby is out into the world, all attention focuses on him. Yet, inside his mom, contractions have not ended. Although they no longer feel like the same contractions experienced moments before, they are occurring. These contractions separate the placenta from the wall of the uterus.

During this time, there are things that you can do to help your body birth your baby.

Things You Can Do for Yourself. Practitioners refer to the muscular action of pushing as bearing down. It is a primal, basic response that you cannot control. Although you may be unsure how to push, you will still have to push with each contraction. You will need to push just as you need to breathe.

Pay close attention to your practitioner and your support people during pushing. They will relay the progress of your baby to you and encourage certain pushes over others. Ask to have a handheld mirror placed where you can see your little one's head emerge from you. This way you can track her progress and witness her arrival.

At first, your practitioner will show you your baby's head way inside of your vagina. It will feel like one step forward and two steps back, as her head comes forward a bit then slips back again. Try not to get discouraged. Eventually, you will see more of her head—and even her hair color.

Once your baby's head stays visible in your vagina, crowning has occurred. Your baby's head will come out and stretch the tissue between your vagina and anus. This area is the perineum. It will burn or sting a bit as the skin fans out to allow your baby's head through. You can sense what the stretching will feel like by placing your thumb and pointer finger on either end of your lower lip and gently pulling the skin outward.

Once baby's entire head is out, you will notice that her face points toward your back. With the next few contractions, her face will magically turn to one of your sides (often your right) so that her shoulders can be born.

During the next few contractions, your practitioner will support your baby's head and help guide your little one right out of you. You can also guide her out yourself. Simply place both hands gently, but firmly around her chest and back, and guide her onto your warm stomach. Don't worry about dropping her. Your practitioner is there to give you a helping hand with her other parts, like her head.

Because pushing is a very physical act, it requires positions that either work with gravity or help a mother use her body to effectively push. Contrary to most current images of birth, this is not achieved with a mother lying on her back. Mothers should be able to give birth in whatever position they choose, unless there is a medical reason this shouldn't happen.

Here is a list of pushing positions that you can try during your baby's birth:

Lying on a Bed in a Semi-Upright Position with Support. This position is quite intimate, since it requires your partner or your doula to sit behind you so that your back leans against his or her chest. If your partner wants to see his baby being born or cut the cord, he might want to switch places with someone else before the birth.

Kneeling on a Bed.   This is a great position to push out a large baby or one with wide shoulders. You can place pillows under your knees or your head for greater comfort. Again, if you have knee problems, choose another position.

Squatting.   Many hospitals and birth centers now have L-shaped bars that attach to the sides of their birth beds that moms can hold on to while squatting. You can also get into a squatting position with the help of two people supporting you. Simply place your arms around the neck of your doula and your partner and dangle your body between them. Give your weight over to them. You can get into this position on the bed, standing, or semisitting. Sometimes it is better to squat for only part of the pushing period since it can be very tiring for the legs.

Side-lying.   Side-lying can feel good after a long and difficult labor. In this position, one leg is flat against the bed, while someone holds your other leg up in the air, often bent at the knee, so that your baby's head can come out. Your partner or doula can hold your leg behind the knee with one hand while you rest your foot in the crook of their other arm.

Classic C Position.   This is the classic position that many moms give birth in. Typically, she will have loads of pillows against her back while she holds her legs up at the knees. The name "C position" comes from the fact that her upper torso is curled into a C shape.

You can move yourself into a variety of these positions alone, but you will probably need the assistance of your partner.

Things Your Partner Can Do.   The father of today is not the bystander at birth, sequestered in the waiting room or at home for the announcement of his baby's sex. Today's father has the option to be right in the thick of things, actually touching his child's head as intimately as the mother does. However, this experience is not something that is available only to fathers. As the concept of what makes a family changes, and mothers choose all sorts of partners for themselves, it is clear that birth transforms everyone connected into a family.

Things Your Doula Can Do.   Your doula will quietly assist you during pushing by counting slowly while you push. Although there is no magic number to reach during pushing, counting acts as a short-term goal that is reachable. Mothers can push for ten full counts and know that once ten is reached, they can pause and rest until the next urge to push hits. Some mothers find counting distracting. They would rather have their doulas wipe their foreheads with a cool cloth and breathe words of encouragement of their baby's progress.

Pushing takes time and physical effort. Since pushing can last for up to two hours, a doula can help a mother remember the intricate dance that is occurring inside her body. Only when the baby is out of the birth canal is the dance complete, although one final stage remains.

THIRD STAGE OF LABOR

The third stage of labor usually goes unnoticed. Unless there is a medical reason why you should be aware of its occurrence, you will blissfully experience quiet contractions that will help separate the placenta from the uterine wall where it implanted like the root of a tree early in the pregnancy. Once it has detached, the placenta will move down the uterus, through the opened cervix, and out of the vagina.

You may be encouraged by your practitioner to gently push it out if you feel it pressing against your cervix. Once it is out, take a peek at it. This amazing organ keeps a baby alive and well throughout most of the pregnancy. It carries nourishment and blood full of oxygen to the baby via the umbilical cord and stores waste products from the baby. It also produces hormones that are essential for the developing baby and the mother. As a barrier, it is an excellent shield against many illnesses that could affect the baby, although viruses can still find their way through it.

Unfortunately, one look at the placenta will tell you none of this. In fact, it looks rather plain. Placentas are disc-like organs that are smooth on one side and bumpy on the other. Blood vessels cover most of its surface.

Physically, and even emotionally, you may be interested in the placenta. Some cultures consider it the baby's twin that should be buried once it has come out. Other mothers bury it somewhere on their property, often planting a tree or a flower on top of it. These small commemorative ideas are ways many mothers celebrate the birth of the baby who has changed them in nine short months.

The labor and birth scenarios that I have described in this chapter have not addressed the fact that sometimes the comfort and caring of a doula, partner, or other loved one does not lessen the anxiety or the discomfort of labor. For many moms, this is when they start to consider the use of pain medication.

What is pain medication, really? And how can it affect experiencing birth holistically?

6

✿ ✿ ✿

NATURAL AND
MEDICAL PAIN RELIEF

So far, I have made little mention of medication to relieve pain. Why? For one important reason: I respect pain medication too much to treat it as a commonplace thing.

Medication affects a mother and her baby and, in rare cases, can cause complications. Should that frighten you? No. Birth is a natural event that can occasionally benefit from medical technology. Unfortunately, technology can also take over and become the focus of birth. A clever spoof of birth is in *The Meaning of Life* by Monty Python. In one scene a mother is giving birth, yet the staff keeps bringing in all of their incredible machines, including the one that goes "ping." Eventually, there is so much equipment in the room that the mother is lost in the chaos. A bit heavy on the symbolism, but the sentiment is quite close to the distance that technology can potentially create during a birth.

Coupled with this idea is the use of pain relief. It can potentially remove a mother from holistically experiencing her baby's birth. Regardless of this potential dissociation, choosing to have pain relief is a personal decision.

Unfortunately, some people do not feel this way. Instead, they tell mothers to forego pain medication or to take it with no middle ground in between. Most of these comments are wrapped up in some notion of the right way to birth a baby. With all of the arguments for or against pain medication, one of the most important questions gets lost in the shuffle: How does an individual mother respond to pain? Without any knowledge of how one responds to pain, the discussion about pain medication has hurtled past a major factor in the equation that has to be evaluated first.

YOUR BODY'S RESPONSE TO PAIN

I have already spoken about listening to your body during labor. This means not only noticing how your uterus tightens during a contraction but also recognizing the way you respond. How you respond can be a good indicator of your perception of the pain of the contractions. Feelings of anxiety and fear can cause the release of stress hormones that make your body think that you are in danger. This can, in turn, force your body to increase your heartbeat, decrease blood flow to the uterus, and give you the sensation that you have a muscle cramp in the very same spot.

Your uterus is a muscle that needs continuous blood flow in order to contract well. Without blood, the muscle becomes starved and can get into an overtaxed contracting pattern that is painful but brings about no progress in labor. The chance of getting into this pattern can be lessened by removing tension from the body, relaxing during labor, and providing the fuel that the uterus may need.

Yet a time may come when a mother feels that her coping mechanisms and her birth team's support is not enough. She may consider taking pain medication.

If you think that you may need something to help reduce pain during labor, you should have it. However, you need to think about this carefully. You have another passenger to consider when you are pondering medication. What affects you affects your baby. And some pain medications affect your baby more than others do. Although your choice should be dictated by your baby's reaction to the medication, you should also choose medication based on what sort of pain lessening you need. But what is pain?

Inside every mother are morphine-like substances called endorphins that naturally block the perception of pain. Every mother has her own pain limit consistent with the levels of endorphins and other chemicals in her body that give her a surge of energy to fight or flee. Such things as sleep, relaxation, and body fuel can also influence a mother's perception of pain. Our earlier discussion of an overtaxed uterus attested to that. However, this does not mean that to feel pain one must be in an unnatural body rhythm. Pain is simply pain. How you tolerate it is another matter.

You know your way of responding to pain. This may or may not affect your perception of pain during labor, but it is something to think about. If you normally respond to a headache by reaching for a bottle of headache reliever, you might want to rethink the way labor will feel for you. If you work hard to control every part of your life because you hate being out of control, you definitely should consider what labor will do to your stress level and, as a result, your perception of pain.

No matter how you perceive pain, plan on dealing with it head-on during labor. Use the many comfort techniques mentioned in this section to help you remain relaxed and comfortable. To recap, here's a list of the natural pain relievers that can be used during labor:

Natural Pain Relievers

Water
How: Tub, shower, frozen washcloth, hot water bottle
- An excellent tension reducer
- Very relaxing

111

- Does not lessen pain but may lessen perception of pain
- Can help labor progress
- Can rejuvenate overstretched, tired muscles

Massage
How: Light touch or deep connection
- Very relaxing
- An excellent tension reducer
- Does not lessen pain but may lessen perception of pain
- Can rejuvenate overstretched, tense muscles
- Can help labor progress

Presence of doula or partner
How: In manner most supportive of mother
- An excellent tension reducer
- Does not lessen pain but may lessen perception of pain
- Can help labor progress

Position
How: See lists in Chapter 5 that describe labor and pushing positions
- An excellent tension reducer
- Can help labor progress
- Does not lessen pain, but may lessen perception of pain

Music, lights, sounds, and scents
How: See ways mentioned in Chapter 5
- Very relaxing
- An excellent tension reducer
- Does not lessen pain but may lessen perception of pain
- Can rejuvenate overstretched, tired muscles
- Can help labor progress

There is also the option of medical pain relief. Many mothers have heard about epidurals, but they are probably unaware that there are other medical pain relief options available during labor. All of these options affect mothers and babies to some extent.

Table 6.1   Types of Medical Pain Relief

Type of Drug	Given by	Tends to be used	Benefits to mom	Concerns for mom or baby
Sedatives Barbiturates	Pill, injection, or IV	During a long labor or active labor	Allows rest	Not a pain reliever; can cause floating or "out of it" feelings in mom; can cause baby to have problems being alert
Tranquilizers Such as Valium	Injection or IV	Early and active labor	Can help relieve anxiety	Not a pain reliever; can cross in high doses to baby and cause baby to have problems being alert
Analgesics Such as Demerol	Injection, IV	Active labor and later	Provides relief of pain without loss of senses	Can cause sleepiness and other "out of it" feelings in mom; can cause baby to have problems being alert or breathing
Anesthetics Regional and general	A variety of methods	From early labor to birth	Localized to complete pain relief; depending on type, mom is either awake or unconscious	Depending on type, none to depressed heart tones and sleepiness in baby

Table 6.1 displays some of the medications that are available for laboring moms, including the type of drug, how it is given, the times when it is usually administered, and the advantages and disadvantages for both mom and baby. Read this chart carefully and discuss each option with your practitioner.

The personal decision whether or not to take pain medication has become embroiled in a social debate. Pain medication and natural birth have joined the larger discussion of a woman's place in the world. This debate of the role of women and mothers in society has now expanded to include personal issues such as whether a mother should stay at home or go to work, put a child in day care or not, and breast-feed or not.

Suddenly, women, who have had to fight over the years for a variety of rights, are now fighting one another for the right to give birth in the way they choose. Even women who are not involved in the debate feel that they need to reflect on it. This is because the women on either side of the issue feel very passionate about their views.

As a health educator interested in maternity care, political and social issues are important to me. However, they all go out the window when I am working with a particular mother and her family as a doula. Once I am with her, her concerns, her wishes, and her needs are the only things that matter.

Where you stand on this debate is up to you to decide. Reflect on all the discussion and then go your own way. Whatever you choose, make it the choice that meets your needs. However, because this is a holistic book, I want you to reflect further on this issue so that you understand how your mind, body, and spirit feel about experiencing the birth of your baby. Of course, you can only do this as an informed consumer.

To show you how to analyze issues from an informed position, I have put together a brief overview of the most common form of pain medication that laboring women seek, the epidural. Read this part carefully and notice the pros and cons for the procedure.

EPIDURALS

There are proponents and opponents of epidurals, even in the medical community.

Some health professionals believe that no mother should have to give birth in pain. They think that it is almost a humanitarian gift to provide relief of pain during childbirth. To those with this mind-set, epidurals are one way to achieve this.

Other health professionals stress that epidurals are just another procedure that can reduce a mother's power and control over her baby's birth. They feel that women are naturally made to have babies. Although epidurals can give relief to a mother who is suffering during birth, this technology introduces something artificial into the birth process, something that can potentially harm a mother and her baby.

Out of both of these views, which is right? Truthfully, both of them.

First, a definition of an epidural: An epidural is the informal name for epidural anesthesia. During an epidural an anesthetic is introduced into the small space next to a mom's spinal cord to eliminate pain. It also lessens sensations, such as urges to urinate and push out your baby. For the drugs (or drug) of the epidural to be given safely, a mom curves her body into a C-shape—either sitting or lying on her side. This opens the space into which the anesthesiologist inserts a hollow needle. Before the needle is inserted, a topical solution is used to numb the skin.

Once the needle is in, a long tube is inserted through it into the space near the spinal column. The needle is then removed while the tube stays in to administer the medication continuously through a drip bag attached to an IV pole. A mom will usually have a catheter inserted into her bladder and be confined to bed.

The Long and Short of It

Today, epidurals have gotten fancy. Mothers now have the option of a one-shot cocktail of pain relievers that lasts for hours, or a self-service pump that allows them to control how much and how often they receive relief. Of course, only hospitals provide epidurals, and not all of them provide the new options.

Regardless of whether a mother faces a snazzy epidural or an old-fashioned one, each carries drawbacks for her.

All epidurals have the potential to slow contractions, deaden the muscles in a mother's legs (temporarily), and make pushing nearly impossible due to the numbing effects of the epidural. Anesthesiologists tell mothers that they are constantly improving an epidural's effectiveness while reducing its potential side effects. Even with all of these improvements, there are a few catches to the "no pain, baby gain" form of relief offered by an epidural.

Not every mom "takes" to the drugs in an epidural in the same way. Anesthesiologists test moms to see how they respond to small amounts of the medication before going ahead with a full epidural.

A mom can experience severe headaches if her spinal cord's protective wall is punctured accidentally during the administration of an epidural. This occurrence is rare, but that's no consolation if it happens to you. You can feel some comfort in knowing that anesthesiologists have immediate treatments for this.

An epidural reduces the pain of contractions but can also lead to what childbirth educators call the domino effect of interventions:

- ✓ Receive an epidural for the pain (as a result, the contractions slow down)
- ✓ Need Pitocin, a medication that stimulates strong contracting (to start labor back up again)
- ✓ Potentially need a vacuum extraction or forceps-assisted delivery (to bring baby out of the birth canal)
- ✓ Need a large episiotomy, a cut to the area between mom's vagina and anus (to help insert the forceps or vacuum extractor around baby's head)

116

✓ At any time during this chain of events, need a cesarean section

On the other hand, epidurals can also be labor savers, allowing contractions to intensify and a mom's body to relax and be in labor. You see, an epidural is not the enemy of birth. It is simply a tool. Many procedures created for or used during childbirth are also tools. They help mothers and babies stay healthy and safe when there are natural and unnatural complications. Used well, an epidural can allow relaxation to happen and let a mother coexist with her contractions in preparation for birth.

The opponents of epidurals feel that the main problem with them is that they are used regardless of medical need. Proponents state that the only "need" required is a mother's wish to have it. What both sides do not realize is that in an informed consent medical system, both of these views can exist side by side. Mothers can obtain accurate information about risks and benefits and then choose the type of care they want. It is possible to have a holistic birth in a variety of locations and situations.

Sometimes mothers need more than just the option of pain medication during labor and birth. As scary as it may be to consider, immediate medical assistance may be indicated. Ideally, the monitoring during pregnancy and labor detects warning signs before they become dangers. Unfortunately, some birth challenges only crop up during labor and birth. If this happens to you, remember that your baby needs you to focus all of your energy on helping her come out as strong and as healthy as possible.

If you know ahead of time about a complication, talk to other mothers who have been through it. You can also seek out specific organizations for more information. A list of groups that provide information, current research facts, and advocacy for families facing a variety of special needs is included in the resource section at the end of this book.

No matter what challenge arises—whether preterm labor or a cesarean section—know that you have a team ready to go the distance with you. Utilize your partner and your doula, if you have chosen to have one, for whatever support you need. (The organization Doulas of North America wants a doula for every mother and so do I.) You deserve to feel supported and nurtured as you bring your baby into the world, no matter what your circumstances may be.

The final part of this chapter looks at a specific challenge that many childbearing women face in the United States today—a cesarean section. Can a mother have a cesarean section and still have a holistic birth? Absolutely. However, there are a number of variables to work through.

CESAREANS

Twenty to twenty-five percent of babies are born by cesarean section in the United States. That number is much higher than it was fifteen to twenty years ago. In some communities, the rate is in the range of 45–50 percent! Why? It would seem that women's bodies have gotten smaller and babies have gotten bigger. But this is not the case. Babies are not weighing substantially more and women, taken as a group, do not need cesareans because they are somehow incapable of giving birth naturally. A number of the reasons touted by health professionals for the increase in cesareans include financial compensation for cesareans versus vaginal deliveries, simple routine use, and in some cases, aesthetic reasons—keeping the vagina tight and firm.

It may surprise you to learn that the medical community has at times advocated certain procedures, for example, an episiotomy, because it was thought to firm up and tighten the perineum, pleasing her male lover. There have also been times when women who labored quietly were considered dignified. In fact, in a recent issue of the *British Medical Journal,* a doctor, in a letter to the editor, stated that "modern obstetrics can offer women . . . predictable options and a dignified childbirth" with a cesarean section.

While I do not wish a cesarean on any mother, simply because it is major surgery, I know that some of the readers of this book will have one. If a cesarean is indicated for emergency or health reasons, then you need to accept the procedure as the safest alternative for you and your baby. If you do not fall into that category and you would like to lower your risk of having a cesarean section, try the following:

Talk to your practitioner.   Ask him or her questions about the number of cesareans in the practice and learn the protocol for certain complications. Make it clear that you aren't trying to enforce a certain outcome; you're simply curious about what the protocols are for certain situations. Specific questions about cesareans should be things like:

✓ Can I have an epidural and be awake?

✓ How much of my pubic hair will need shaving for the surgery?

✓ Can my partner be with me throughout the operation? What about my doula?

✓ What kind of abdominal incision will I have?

✓ Could I have a vaginal birth in a future pregnancy?

✓ How much pain medication will I need after surgery?

✓ Will I still be able to nurse my baby?

✓ How long will I need to recover?

Avail yourself of your doula.   Clinical trials show that having a doula during labor and birth can significantly reduce the chances of having a cesarean. That does not mean that a doula can prevent complications from happening.

119

Think of birth as something to be experienced instead of something to be conquered.   Modern moms have a tendency to ignore the fact that birth is a physical, emotional, and frequently unpredictable event. Try not to forget that as you prepare yourself for the big day.

Keep a keen eye on the list of interventions used during your labor.   The domino effect of intervention shows that as more interventions are used during birth, the natural patterns and rhythms of labor become more disrupted. Without any of its own resources to fall back on, the body can become unresponsive to its own triggers. Keep trying to respond to your body's natural rhythms and you are one step closer to eliminating the risk of a cesarean.

Read up on cesareans.   Analyze some of the excellent women's health books that discuss issues like a woman's access to health care, the benefits of informed consent, and the holistic needs of pregnant mothers like yourself.

The best-case scenario just before a cesarean birth is that a mother and her partner have discussed things with each other, their doula, and their practitioner and have come to the conclusion that a cesarean is the best choice at the time.

During a cesarean, the main action occurs in a mother's lower abdomen. Thankfully, a screen is arranged to block a mother's view of the surgery. Partners, who are often sitting beside the mother, can look if they want. (Be warned: It is surgery. If your partner does not like the sight of blood, tell him not to look!)

A small incision is made through the abdominal muscles, and another through the lower band of uterine muscles. The incision is so small that the baby seems unlikely to fit through it. The doctor squeezes the baby through the opening and out into the world. Once out, the doctor cuts the baby's umbilical cord. The baby is whisked naked to a nearby table, and as long as he is breathing fine, returned to mom and her partner in a warm blanket. A quick doula tip: Do not forget to bring your glasses. Have your partner stick them in his shirt. That way, when you get your first glimpse of your baby, he won't look like a fuzzy bundle.

The doctor then cleans out the uterus, removing the placenta. There's relatively little blood on mom. A supercharged vacuum-like suction removes any fluid from the uterus into containers positioned under the bed. The final step for the doctor: closing the incisions.

The doctor painstakingly closes the uterus and the abdomen with stitches that are absorbed by the mother's body. Once finished, mom is monitored for a while and then brought to the postpartum floor. If she was not awake for the cesarean, she is moved to a surgical recovery room where every vital sign is carefully evaluated and monitored before she can move to the postpartum floor.

This simple-sounding surgery takes time to recover from because the muscles in the abdomen were cut and then stitched back together. For the first few weeks, coughing will be difficult to do without a pillow against the stitches, and walking will be slow. Mothers are encouraged by the nurses in the hospital to both cough and walk in the first couple of days after the surgery. If progress is slow initially, they have plenty of time to work on it. Hospitals in the United States are legally required to keep a mother who has had a cesarean section in the hospital for ninety-six hours as a minimum.

Length of recovery will depend on the type of incision. The classic bikini cut done in the pubic hairline is the most popular and, incidentally, the one most favorable for a later vaginal birth after cesarean.

CESAREAN SECTION PREP

More happens in preparation for a cesarean. A mother's pubic hair is shaved low to allow the bikini cut through the abdominal muscles. This shaving doesn't hurt, but you may itch like crazy when the hair grows back around the healing incision.

Since most moms are awake, an epidural is given. This loss of sensation also means that going to the bathroom is out of the question. A catheter is inserted into the bladder just before or after the epidural is given. The final preparation for the cesarean is a liberal application of antiseptic over and around the entire abdominal region.

Once a mother returns home, she is on her own, needing to take care of her baby and herself. Recovering from surgery is infinitely easier with help. As soon as you anticipate a cesarean is in your future, seek help. Partners, family members, and even postpartum doulas are available to aid you in your recovery and to care for your baby.

Once birth is complete, motherhood really begins. The first moments with your new baby in your arms signal the start of an amazing new chapter in your life.

Holistic birth is just the start of holistic living and parenting. The final chapters of this book outline many of the mental, physical, and spiritual questions, concerns, and challenges new parenthood brings.

Part Three

❋ ❋ ❋

EMBRACING MOTHERHOOD

With all of the interest in having babies that women exhibit, one would assume that the tricky act of raising and caring for them and the challenges and changes inherent in motherhood would bear equal scrutiny. It does to some extent. Dr. Spock and Penelope Leach have written oodles of books about the development of babies. But what about mothers? Where are the books that delve into their mental, physical, and spiritual changes, concerns, and questions? A quick bookstore scan shows that this information is limited at best and often focuses narrowly on sociopolitical issues of motherhood versus frank discussions of the role itself.

The clear, concise books on postpartum for mothers can be counted on one hand. *After the Baby's Birth* by Robin Lim remains a favorite of mine, as well as *Mothering the New Mother* by Sally Placksin, and nearly everything by British author Sheila Kitzinger. But where are the stories from mothers to other mothers? Where are their empowering voices, guiding the scores of women after them into motherhood? In a word, muted.

Naomi Wolf, author of *The Beauty Myth,* recently joined the motherhood set and produced a book about it. Called *Misconceptions,* the book's basic premise is that women have been forced to navigate their own way through childbearing in America, within a system that continues to treat them as if they are unworthy of respectful care that places their thoughts and goals at the center of its services. She uses her own pregnancy as a starting point and then includes thoughts from friends and medical specialists.

As an examination of health care from the perspective of an educated, self-described feminist, the book is illuminating. Wolf articulates her complex thoughts and unfolding identity as a mother. Written as an examination of her monthly development, Wolf takes the reader on an incredible personal journey of discovery through nine long months and the birth itself. But only three chapters discuss what turns out to be her most challenging time, postpartum.

Amazingly, Wolf is not alone in finding postpartum challenging. Countless mothers find themselves entering a "no woman zone" during postpartum, reading countless books about what to expect only to find themselves ill prepared and unsure of the many changes that they experience. Counsel with their friends turns up more questions. Talking to a doctor or midwife seems impractical, since many mothers perceive they need less, not more, care from their practitioners now that their babies are born.

Who sees the mother's postpartum period as the beautiful, mystical, magical, emotionally chaotic experience that it is, and gives dedicated time and attention in a mother's home to cultivate that experience? Many talented and trained people. High on my list of trusted helpers are postpartum doulas.

These individuals, focused primarily on the postpartum experience of mothers, see pregnancy and birth as critical moments that, upon completion, signal the start, not the end, of a mother's parenting journey. They know that, contrary to popular opinion, things may get harder, not easier, for a mother once her baby is born. Add trying to become a parent in a society that gives only tenuous support to mothers, not to mention a mother's own internal changes as she struggles or embraces her new role, and you have a period of adjustment that can take months rather than days to navigate.

As attendants who see mothers periodically during pregnancy before reuniting after birth, postpartum doulas arrive in a new family's life just when professional support and practical wisdom is needed the most. For most moms, home may be where the heart is, but it is also the one place that they may be unready to return to with their newborns.

The list of things to "watch out for" on returning home with a newborn cannot even compare to the irrational fears a mother may have. These fears can be compounded by a mother's own feelings of inadequacy and even loss. Gone is the woman she was before her baby was born. In her place stands a mother. Who or what that is to each woman depends on the motherhood models she has seen and her philosophy of motherhood. This is something that can take months, even years to discover. This may even impact a mother's biology. According to Sarah Hrdy, in her book *Mother Nature*, "fetal cells have been known to linger on in the mother's body for as long as twenty-seven years" (p. 94).

What ideas do you have about motherhood? In your dreams of life with your newborn, how does your family adjust to a new member? What aspects of mothering do you feel are essential? Breast-feeding? Cloth diapering? Transporting your baby in a carrier or a sling? And what about yourself? Your relationship with your partner? How will all of these things change and merge as your baby grows during infancy and beyond?

All of these questions point to the inner mind, body, and spirit of a new mother. By learning ways to adjust and sustain these core parts of yourself, your evolving identity can truly reflect the mother, the parent, and the partner that you want to be.

Postpartum doulas assist in this growth and development. Full of practical ideas, armed with community resources, and willing to "show" baby and mother care basics, postpartum doulas act as guides or perhaps simply illuminators of the journey into motherhood that is yours alone to make.

Many postpartum doulas feel that they are reviving the culturally dead practice of women sustaining women within the community, which used to be a cornerstone of childbearing. If you need this kind of personal care and comfort, find a postpartum doula in your community.

But don't stop there. Continue reading this book and others for information, ideas, and advice that can turn motherhood into a realistically doable experience, rather than a fantasy of idealized proportions.

In Part 3 I aim to go beyond the standard postpartum discussion to shine a strong light of honesty and practicality on the parenting process. Arranged in three easy-to-follow chapters, Part 3 demystifies and answers many of the questions about motherhood.

What is ultimately left up to you is how you let this information strengthen or sustain your belief and your identity as a mother. Motherhood is a time of change and transformations, but it is also a time of blessings. Embrace all that the experience offers: the happiness, the aches, and the joy.

7

❈ ❈ ❈

YOUR BALANCED MIND

A new mother's body and spirit have to adjust and develop throughout her motherhood journey, but it is perhaps her mind that faces the greatest challenge. There, issues thrive and start to potentially create depression, blues, and mood disorders, which can hinder the developing relationship with a new baby.

From the first day of becoming a mother, a woman finds herself battling her own insecurities while creating a motherhood identity that is hers and hers alone. Even with the barrage of visitors and advice givers, she may still wake up periodically in the night and wonder where she fits into all these changes. Within a matter of hours, she has been transformed into a full-fledged mother, complete with anxiety attacks and immense responsibility. Coupled with plummeting pregnancy hormones and rising breast-feeding hormones, she becomes a mass of needs, crises, and joy. At nearly no other time in a mother's life is the fragility and complexity of her moods and her thoughts so intertwined with her hormones. Similar to the changes that occur just before a woman's menstrual cycle and during menopause, the hormones of a new mother are coursing fast and furious in a spiral of adaptations that can propel even the most grounded mother into a bit of a blue mood.

Mood concerns notwithstanding, new mothers face a torrent of other issues, challenges that become more pronounced the moment they return home after a hospital or birth center birth, or settle into their home life once the highs of a home birth have worn off.

With the loss of the rose-colored glasses, many mothers wake up to the reality that their lives are no longer their own. Throughout this time, certain mental signs or patterns may start to emerge; things they should listen or pay attention to for continued stability and health.

MENTAL PATTERNS

The first time a new mother walks into her house with her baby, she is often amazed at the changes in her family, blessed to have a baby so adorable, and swamped by questions and doubts of her ability to care for her baby for the next hour and eventual years. For a time, her world seems not only immensely challenging but also downright otherworldly. Her body, her life, her partner, her baby, and her family are all in a state of flux.

Unfortunately, our society does not recognize these kinds of thoughts and feelings. Ask people who are not mothers about the first days and weeks postpartum, and they will tell you that women walk around in a haze of maternal brightness and excitement. This myth of maternal bliss convinces many mothers they must have something wrong with them, since they did *not* rise up from their birth bed, grab a semiskim latté, and step out into the world with their babies on their backs.

This is not the experience of every mother, though. Some moms feel a high level of trust and awareness after birth that makes them feel strong and purposeful. They know who they are and where they are going as a mother, and nothing anyone says is going to make them doubt their abilities.

The mothers who are superconfident and assured are not the norm. Studies tell us that many new moms experience anxiety about their abilities to mother a vulnerable newborn, and are swamped with swinging moods and fluctuating desires.

Current research states that nearly 80 percent of new mothers will face some oscillation in their moods. Alternately called the baby blues or postpartum blues, these feelings are not akin to a blues song on the radio. Feelings of inadequacy and swinging moments of crying and exhaustion can characterize this time. Although this is often blamed on hormonal changes, little is known about the exact cause. In fact, little is known psychologically about many of the concerns women encounter that revolve around their reproductive hormones.

Two researchers and clinicians who are trying to change this long-standing trend are Dr. Deborah Sichel and Jeanne Driscoll, a psychotherapist and nurse. Coauthors of the book *Women's Moods,* these two are sounding the call to mothers and health professionals alike to start paying attention to the mental health patterns that are a part of each of us. Their plea comes at a most fortunate time, given the national attention focused on a couple of terrible events that unfolded under the alleged haze of postpartum disorders.

The intense brain focusing that Driscoll and Sichel advocate allows mothers to recognize things about themselves that are a product of their lifelong brain formation. Although many mothers may not have experienced mental illnesses, their bodies, and notably their brains, know plenty about stress and anxiety. Driscoll and Sichel talk openly in their book about the problems facing many mothers who interact with a maternity system that has their well-being in mind but is often ill informed about how to specifically help. It is only through researchers like Sichel and Driscoll that health professionals today understand that more in-depth analysis needs to be given when a mother experiences a moment of the blues.

Characterized on television shows and in movies as crying bouts that occur for no reason, as well as moments of yelling and distraction that make conversation difficult, the "baby blues" describes a period of adjustment that affects each mother differently. Some, who have adequate support and assistance, may only feel slightly distracted and moody. For them, blue feelings disappear soon after birth. Other mothers, especially those who are exhausted and unsupported during the early weeks of parenthood, are more prone to feel the blues intensely.

This should not come as a surprise. Support and rest have a profound affect on a mother's emotional and mental state. For more evidence of this, reflect on your own life for a moment. What happens to you in the middle of your menstrual cycle or just before your flow starts? You may be one of the many women who experience hormonal fluctuation that precipitates psychological changes commonly called PMS. Although jokes have abounded for years about the severity and the reality of any premenstrual syndromes, the truth is that many women undergo mental changes that challenge them just before or after their period. The severe form of this physical and emotional disturbance is called premenstrual dysphoric disorder. Known mostly as PMDD, this new classification of severe PMS is only recently getting attention by the media and by women. Treatment for PMDD and PMS often includes lifestyle changes.

A new mother can battle the baby blues using many of the same self-help techniques. Not surprisingly, many of the suggested self-care ideas are included in this book as ways to create a positive life. It seems once again that living a healthy, balanced life can have profound effects.

There are also other ways to reduce the effects of the blues.

Ways to Lower the Effects of Postpartum Blues

Sleep when needed. You will feel better and mentally spring from action to reaction quicker. Sleeping will also help refuel your emotions and sustain your physical strength.

Eat a balanced diet. Starving your body or delaying eating only makes it harder for you to process and accomplish mental tasks and complete physically demanding jobs like caring for your new baby. A body that has to work overtime to do the simplest things can get into a state of distress, compounding mental and physical concerns with fatigue. For your mental health, eat well and eat healthy.

Surround yourself with supportive people. Nothing is worse during the early days postpartum than to be surrounded by people who say unsupportive things and offer little or no help caring for a restless newborn. Look at your support team. From your doula to your partner, talk frankly with everyone about what you need from them and how they can work together to help you. Doulas do this kind of work actively since it is part of their game plan. Partners and other family members may need a little push in the right direction in order to offer you the assistance and comfort that you need. Take time to address your concerns with those you trust in the most nonconfrontational manner that you can summon. Their support and assistance during this time not only is helpful but may be psychologically necessary. Women who enter motherhood alone are more inclined to confront moments of insecurity and anxiety.

Reduce caffeine, sugar, and alcohol. Many mothers look to these three things as security blankets. They reach for one or all of these items to lessen tension, reduce anxiety, or make feelings of sadness go away. But anyone who actually experiences mood disturbances such as postpartum blues needs to avoid these substances in order to ensure that their bodies are not battling chemicals that may interfere with the body's other biochemical interactions. The swings that sugar, alcohol, and caffeine provide are clearly apparent. If you find that you cannot give up your favorite items, figure out ways to lessen your dependency on them or choose an alternative. Decaffeinated coffee, nonalcoholic beer, and sugar substitutes exist that actually taste good.

Exercise.   Moderate exercise, even something as simple as walking, can do wonders for a mother's body and mood. Studies consistently suggest mood improvement among those who exercise regularly. One 2001 study in the *Journal of Sports Medicine and Physical Fitness* demonstrated that anger, tension, confusion, and fatigue were reduced by exercise while vigor, a term that connotes energy and vitality, increased.

But many mothers find themselves experiencing something beyond simple mood swings or blue periods. Current estimates suggest that 10–20 percent of new mothers will undergo major depression after birth, known as postpartum depression. This category is found in the *Diagnostic and Statistical Manual of Mental Disorders—Fourth Edition (DSM-IV)* published by the American Psychiatric Association. This bible of mental health has only recently recognized the various reproductive concerns facing women. It is hoped that with the more vocal public awareness of the patterns of mood disorders facing many women, there will no longer be 0.1–0.2 percent of mothers who battle severe and traumatic postpartum psychosis, a disorder that can include thoughts of suicide, infanticide, and hallucinations.

Luckily, many mood disorders are treatable with medication or therapy. However, something else needs to happen in our country for new mothers to overcome these disorders and patterns of insecurities. First off, new mothers need to be surrounded by supportive people who strive to do little else but mother them. Far too often, mothers start their first few days with their babies attended by overworked, understaffed professionals who cannot devote countless hours to them. This has to change for mothers to feel cared for. Birth facilities need to staff more people so that more mothers feel cherished and comforted during those first tenuous hours with their babies.

Something else also needs to happen. Health professionals need to be trained to listen and respond to the many concerns of new mothers. Studies suggest that many mothers are so embarrassed by nonmaternal feelings after birth that they keep them to themselves, often prolonging periods of anxiety and distress.

You too may have thoughts, feelings, or concerns that seem to rise up from some dark corner in your mind. Talk to someone about what you are struggling with. If you are not ready to share with a professional, talk openly with your partner, your doula, a religious adviser, or a friend. Make sure that someone is listening to your many thoughts and feelings as you strive to make sense of your world and your altered position within it.

One critical thing that you can do for yourself postpartum is reflect on the ways that you have trained yourself to respond to stress, anxiety, and change. We considered this briefly in the birth section, but the tenets of the subject ring just as true for the postpartum period as well. How you have learned to deal with certain stressful or chaotic situations is often a good indication of how you may respond to pregnancy, birth, and the many changes of postpartum. In *Women's Moods,* Sichel and Driscoll discuss certain clients who came to them after experiencing postpartum depression. They did not have a history of mental episodes in their lives yet described a parent's death or another trauma in their past.

Although I am not suggesting that something traumatic has happened to you and will color your experience of motherhood, I know some "things" have transpired over the years to help create you. How you were forged says a lot about the type of mother you will be, and the gates or hurdles that you may have to journey through in order to align all the parts of yourself into one cohesive whole.

If your mental patterns suggest that you may be at risk for depression or may have trouble adjusting to the isolation or loss of freedom that motherhood can trigger, you need to immediately do a number of things for your mental health and safety. First, talk to your practitioner. Although some doctors and midwives are uninformed about the various treatments and current information on mood disorders, most are earnestly interested in helping mothers cope with alterations to their lives. If, after talking to your doctor or midwife about your thoughts and feelings, you still do not feel that you are being heard or helped, seek out another women's health professional or support person. With the current massive interest in alternative therapies has come a renewed dedication to healing the mind, body, and spirit of a patient. Many practitioners actively strive to heal the whole person; there are also mental health therapists who work specifically with women and women's issues.

As a consumer, you deserve to receive health care that is responsive, appropriate, and respectful of your needs. Even though mental health issues are not as front and center in the nation's consciousness as they should be, you should never have to settle for second-class service when it comes to your health and mental well-being.

Of course, your partner is in many ways more critical as a confidante than your doula or your practitioner. Your mate or partner is the person who is there for you and with you throughout this entire journey of parenthood. How you deal with and handle this evolving partnership matters immensely to both your enjoyment of motherhood and your relationship with this loved one.

Your relationship with your partner impacts your life in many ways. The more in tune you are with him, the better, and in many ways the more stable your parenting journey will be. In essence, the two of you need each other for support and encouragement. But you also need each other for companionship and love. It is possible to forget that when all of your energy is spent raising and caring for a newborn. Parenting a newborn is so exhausting and consuming that many new mothers lose sight of their partners and themselves.

Losing or forgetting your connection with your partner can affect you mentally on many levels. This disconnection can have profound effects on your enjoyment of mothering and your satisfaction with yourself, since your identity as a woman and a mother is often impacted by your relationship with others—especially your partner.

Staying connected and joined with your mate is only part of the equation, since you also have to figure out how to work together. The new mothers I have counseled consistently remark about feeling frustrated as they watch their egalitarian relationship turn into a "he does this, she does that" situation that is not based on equality or fairness. How then can you reclaim the shared relationship with your partner that you had before the pregnancy and continue to build your intimacy as a couple? By making your partnership one that is important enough to work at every day.

Splitting the Load

Noted sociologist Arlie Hochschild, in her landmark study on two-career parents, found that while a couple may elect to split their home-life responsibilities evenly, something happens once a baby is born that transforms this lovingly neutral relationship into a sex-specific role play. The hardest-hit moms are often the career women who thought they had found an equal partner to love and work beside. Whether the gender-specific duties that men and women assume once they have a family are a product of our society's moldings or are a natural expression of the separation of the sexes is immaterial, since many women who express a desire for things to be more equal continue to take on most of the work load at home while caring for their babies and, in many cases, working. Hochschild refers to this women's work as the second shift, the title of her book recounting the study.

What is your situation? Have you and your partner decided to split things or are you taking on everything? During the early weeks after birth, there are many, many people around who are able to help care, cook, and clean. Once this group leaves you, a plan of action needs to be implemented. If you plan to return to work soon after the birth of your baby, this organization becomes imperative. Otherwise, you will end up doing what many women do: cook, clean, work, parent, volunteer for everything, and find yourself stressed, overworked, and just plain tired. I see many mothers of young babies who are trying to find some balance in their world but are struggling under a weight of significant demands.

While you may be able to juggle many things at the same time, why do it when you have decided to parent a child with your partner? When you realize how difficult parenting is, it becomes clear that the most important thing you can do is go at it together, not as identical models but as a joined force. What if your idea of parenting does not match your partner's? It is possible and likely that, even though the two of you may be compatible as lovers and friends, you have completely different ideas about raising a baby. We'll talk more about parenting, but for now note that your partner is more than just a warm body. This is the person you have hopefully chosen to raise a baby with and, in many cases, spend the rest of your life with as a couple.

This means that from now on, decisions that affect your baby are made together. With the arrival of your baby came the incomprehensible and intricate task of parenting a being into an adult. Do your relationship a favor by keeping your focus on your family. This tight unit should be the center of the world. Everything else on the outside, even your career and his career, is not as critical as the love of your family. It is there that dreams are made, magic is formulated, and hope for the future is sustained.

If you are in a relationship that is dangerous, unhealthy, or weakened, for the sake of your baby and your mental health, get help. No child and no woman should live a life of fear or danger. As for love? It is my greatest wish when I work with a family that each member within it is touched by love. Can you imagine how the world would look if families spread love?

The traumatic acts of terrorism that recently rocked the country have prompted many families to work harder to express and feel love. Many have a renewed interest in hope. It is for the mental health of everyone that mothers, fathers, and other family members strive to embrace the future. Looking into the eyes of a baby will prove that this task is well worth it.

For some mothers, though, their biggest worry is becoming like their mothers. They have flashes of their mothers throughout their pregnancies and well into their babies' infancies. They either want to be like them or feel despair that they will be. Either way, they are filled with fear or trepidation.

What is it about the women in our direct matrilineal line that inspires such emotion? Is it because so many mothers, such as yourself, are members of the club of 1 million children since 1972 who have seen their parents divorce? Perhaps. The self-help titles that fill any bookstore show title after title devoted to surviving divorce as an adult and learning how to manage and handle relationships. This condition affects more than just a mother's (or a father's) notion of relationships with a partner. It also colors how they conceptualize parenthood. New mothers who have witnessed abusive relationships, career-minded overworked mothers, and neglectful fathers as their models of parenthood find themselves struggling with insecurities as they strive to find in themselves the parent that they feel their baby deserves. But this may not have been your experience. Your parents may be wonderful, kind, loving people who are still together. Regardless of their temperament and behavior, they have helped shape your parenting ideals.

Look at your parenting models. Do you feel that your mother did the best she could given her situation? What about your father? Are you still harboring feelings of frustration about things that you feel they did to you? What about the way they raised you? Are there things that you now wish they would have done to help you as a baby? Consider these questions but try not to brood on them. Your goal is only to understand what may be motivating some of your own parenting goals.

And you have parenting goals. In your mind, there is an image of the mother you think you should be. For better or worse, this mental model fuels your actions on behalf of your baby. How realistic is the model? Is it something, or rather someone, that you really want to become? Why? Because she is so similar (or not) to your own mother?

Thinking about their parents is something many new mothers can't help but do. They start their first few days postpartum with their mothers, fathers, or in-laws nearby. Sometimes these relationships are strained by the stress and uncertainty of new parenthood. If it is better for you mentally, consider having your parental figures come later, after you and your family have established some sort of rhythm. This may help you focus your mental energies where they belong in the first few days after birth: on your baby. This does not mean that you should forget about your parents and other family members. Just after birth is a good time to ponder the familial ties that you have established. These people will undoubtedly play an important part in your baby's life. Your relationship with them may impact the relationship that your baby establishes now and later. As with so many things, you can control what type of atmosphere this connection will occur in, at least on your part.

As you process your emotions about these family members, factor in one major thing: Parenthood and "familyhood" come without any directions for parents or signs that they have done a good job. The fears that many mothers have of becoming like their mothers are, in many cases, based on the very real potential of teaching what they have been taught. Although being conditioned by your parents is not a guarantee, there is plenty of evidence that we often repeat what we know. What do you do if you want to bring about a change in parenting for your baby but have no models to emulate? Talk to your postpartum doula. Postpartum doulas are primary modelers of ways to care for and be with a newborn, often showing mothers by example the ways that they can choose to interact with their infants. I tell many new mothers that doulas assure and buffer the core parts of a mother so that she can tap into a wellspring of good feelings for her new role. It is this type of support that allows a mother to give her baby what she is receiving: positive energy. When a mother receives nothing but negative vibes and negative words about her mothering ability from the people she sees as her family, her perception of herself is affected. Gone is her belief that what she is doing is the best she can for her baby. In its place is the conviction that she may be doing the "wrong" thing for the health and future of her child.

Although some actions, such as shaking a baby, are clearly wrong, many parenting techniques do not come with a guarantee of working. For example, despite the media assertions of the glowing effects of Mozart music listening, parents who play Mozart for their babies are not guaranteed to grow a smarter baby. The initial research on Mozart's music, dubbed the Mozart Effect, was done with adults. Subsequent research done with children found an amazing growth in spatial temporal reasoning but little change in IQ. Another study done after children learned to play piano music by Mozart claimed that they improved in mathematics.

What does this mean for your baby? Little. It mainly means that there are many things you can try to help you parent your baby. Evaluate each one carefully before doing anything. Understand the difference between what your baby needs and what you would like your baby to have or do in order to be pretty, perfect, and prepared for the world.

What am I alluding to? Take a walk through any infant area in a department store. Many of the items for sale are of interest to parents rather than babies. From strollers with matching coverlets to baby sneakers in miniature adult styles, baby items have become commodities, things that express the style of parents more than meet babies' needs. Why am I mentioning this? Because the type of parent you want to be must stay independent of these things.

Parenthood is hard enough without losing sight of the practical side of it all. Here is a list of practical must do's and must have's for any mother's mental sanity.

The Practical List

Practice time management. For a brief period after your baby's birth, you will have no concept of time. Hours will flow in and out of your life as you struggle with sleep deprivation and your newborn's needs. Eventually, though, you will strike a balance with your baby (at least until his next growth spurt) and have a clear sense of what you need to do next.

Become a certified time manager by utilizing your time efficiently. This does not mean learn how to do everything at the same time. Instead, the goal is to reflect on what needs to be done and then arrange your life to suit your needs. If more playtime is desired, plan that. If more reading time is needed, plan that. It may be a simple approach, but I believe that we get back in our lives the very thing that we strive for. If you truly want to enjoy your family and your partner, you will find a way to do that. Otherwise, you will sense what happens when your priorities are fragmented. You tend to become fragmented too.

Set up a life for yourself outside of your family. Make your family the center of your world, but take the time to give yourself something more. Choose a hobby, a course, or a ritual just for yourself. Give yourself this time to reflect on nothing but your thoughts, dreams, and desires. As fulfilling as motherhood is, it is only a part of the person that you have become. Think of it this way: What type of woman do you want your child to see years from now when she looks at you? That woman is inside you now. Cultivate her. Love her. Let her grow.

Resist the urge to know everything. Although I am glad that you are reading this book to learn more ways to embrace motherhood, I must caution you not to wish, plan, or plot all of this wondrous experience. As curious as my mind is about many of the things that affect mothers, fathers, and families, I respect the magic that is a part of the parenthood journey. There are indescribable moments of joy and humor when parents are literally humbled by their babies. Nothing—no book or person— can prepare you for the moments of startling emotion that can overcome parents while looking at their baby and recognizing their little one's wisdom and strength. Allow yourself the quiet moments to feel this with your child.

Enjoy every moment. Being a parent is the hardest job in the world. Respect that, and you will give yourself fewer worries. Parenting is confusing, challenging, beautiful, and a blessing. And as a parent, you are a blessing. Where would your baby be without you? He needs you, just as the world does. With your worldview as a mother, you are able to see dimensions and solutions to problems that are both big and small. No wonder there is a famous saying that the world would be a better place if mothers ran it.

This practical approach to surviving parenting and the patterns of your mind is also useful the first time you stare at your body after birth. The form that you have come to recognize as yourself looks completely different. Yet, even in its current state of flux, your body is beautiful.

8

❊ ❊ ❊

YOUR BEAUTIFUL BODY

Mothers everywhere stare at their postpregnant selves in amazement and just a touch of panic. Nothing looks like it used to. Breasts that were just starting to appear "normal" in their swollen, fecund state, swell even further in preparation for nursing. While this can be disconcerting, it's not nearly as odd as the deflated-balloon look of a new mother's belly.

She may have thought she would enter postpartum with a flat stomach, but that doesn't happen. And to top it off, the uterus continues to contract, forcing small amounts of blood out of the vagina for up to six weeks—even if a mother has had a cesarean!

The body, in its amazing compartmentalized form, takes a mother into motherhood whether or not she is mentally ready.

Some mothers perceive these changes as evidence of their goddess status—only someone powerful could carry a baby, give birth to her, and then be able to keep her alive with nothing but her body. But many women are shocked by their appearance and do not experience this positive physical image.

They may even feel that a virtual stranger is masquerading in their stretched skin.

This shock is surprising given the proliferation of childbirth classes, birth videos, and pregnancy-related books. Even with all of the interest in birth and parenting, there remains very little information about the physical alterations a new mother undergoes; and she is a mother, even if she cannot quite call herself that.

Look at your body. During middle or advanced pregnancy, your body alters its shape and design for the benefit of your baby. As you gaze at yourself now, take in your swollen breasts, distended belly, and feet. Work hard within your mind to visualize these changes as powerful, positive signs of the hard work of motherhood—not weight gain or fat. We women spend incredible amounts of time obsessing about weight. Even books and movies with strong heroines and no-nonsense women portray characters who obsess about almost every item they consume. And these women are not alone. A quick scan of the most popular pregnancy-related Web sites for postpartum information shows a plethora of articles devoted mostly to losing weight after birth.

While I encourage every mother to eat healthy foods, I think that it is unhealthy to focus only on losing weight. By dwelling only on dieting, the many amazing and confusing things happening to a woman's body become ignored. And you shouldn't ignore these changes. You should discover them.

DISCOVERING WHAT'S IN
THE MIDDLE OF YOUR BODY

The Uterus

As soon as a baby comes out of the birth canal, attention shifts in the birthing room from the mother to her baby. For the mother, the birth of her baby signals another, quiet birth of change inside her body. Never is that change clearer than in the moments after the expulsion of the placenta.

Immersed in the world of their new babies, exhausted and often sleep deprived, mothers are simultaneously bewildered and amazed at the feeling within their womb when they put their baby to the breast to suckle. For brief moments, they get a glimpse of what is happening inside.

The uterus, the hollow, thick muscular organ that acts as your baby's house, stretches to considerable size during pregnancy like a dangling balloon. Kept in place by a number of ligaments between your bladder and your rectum, your uterus is truly the most amazing organ in your body. You only get a small peek at its existence each month leading up to and during menstruation. The slight discomfort, enlargement of the uterine wall, and eventual discharge of blood at the end of the cycle does not adequately describe the intuitive, centuries' old adaptations the uterus knows how to make.

This same innate knowledge transforms the pregnant uterus immediately after baby's birth into its new, postpregnancy form. Still enlarged, the uterus needs to contract firmly in order to close the uterine blood vessels that were torn with the removal of the deeply implanted placenta. This area of blood leakage is large. The placenta, weighing about 450 grams, is a circular organ that is close to twenty centimeters in diameter.

While the strong postbirth contractions shunt the bleeding vessels off, they also expel blood. The body, inherently smarter than anyone gives it credit for, expels this blood in small amounts. Any copious blood loss of more than two cups is typically a sign of postpartum hemorrhage. Practitioners, no matter where they provide birth services, immediately take steps to remedy this potentially dangerous situation.

The typical blood flow after birth, you recall, can last up to six weeks. During this time, you might notice moments when the blood is heavy and even has small clots within it. If you find either of these things happening postpartum, stop what you are doing and put your feet up for a bit. Small clots, although often nothing to worry about, can appear when a mother has physically exerted herself too much. Resting usually results in the return of normal flow.

A WARNING SIGN

Heavy blood loss and continued clotting are both signs that mothers need to address immediately with a doctor or midwife so that they can assess the situation.

Postpartum blood flow, referred to medically as lochia, is also affected by breast-feeding. When a newborn suckles at its mother's breast, a hormone is released that causes the uterus to tighten and squeeze out blood. This means that in addition to regular blood flow after birth, there may be moments of additional gushing during breast-feeding. This is usually not anything to be concerned about.

During the first weeks postpartum, keep large, absorbent menstrual or obstetrical pads throughout the house. Create a number of storage places throughout your house that contain products you may need for your healing body. Storing absorbent pads upstairs in your bathroom almost guarantees that you will need one when you are downstairs in the kitchen cooking dinner. To lessen a chance of leaking on your clothing, change pads often. A soaked pad is not only an opportunity for leakage, it is also a breeding ground for bacteria.

Postpartum blood loss sounds like an excruciating ordeal, but it is relatively uneventful and often short. The lochia stage lasts as long as it takes the uterus to return to its prepregnant size and position, deep in the pelvis, tucked behind the pubic bone felt in your pubic hair. You can monitor this change by feeling for the top, or fundus, of the uterus.

Within moments of birth, the top of the uterus feels like the curve of a grapefruit. You can check this yourself and relate progress to your postpartum nurse or your practitioner. Involution, the medical name for the return of the uterus to its prepregnant size, never completely returns this versatile organ to its former state. Just as the rest of you has been irrevocably changed by pregnancy, so too has the uterus.

It continues to weigh about forty grams, but the inside is wider and the muscular layers and other parts more weathered, bearing the physical evidence of the amazing journey into parenthood that the rest of your body has undertaken.

Stretch Marks

One surreal glance at your skin will show stretch marks, those delicious dark or silvery marks where the skin grew quickly and scarred. No matter what magical cream or fantasy rub you try, you cannot rid yourself of stretch marks. It is a hereditary thing often compounded by maternal or infant size.

If it makes you feel better to think you are doing something to prevent stretch marks, rub your belly with whatever lotion you want, as long as it doesn't dry out your skin or cause an allergic reaction. Better yet, have your partner do it for you. It may not reduce your chances of getting stretch marks, but it sure will feel good.

Stretch marks, though, may be the least of your concerns as you take in your stretched skin. Mothers who have had large babies or multiples may find that their skin has stretched so much that it may hang slightly during the early weeks postpartum.

Even mothers who had an average-size baby may find that their skin looks wrinkled. Once the elastic skin rebounds into shape, the wrinkles should disappear. Sudden weight gain and lack of exercise can reduce the body's chances of tightening this extra skin.

Postpartum Fitness

The American College of Obstetricians and Gynecologists (ACOG) revised its guidelines on exercise to support women who have maintained an exercise regime to resume their active lifestyle based on their own body timetable. It may have taken ACOG decades to get with it, but they are essentially telling women to listen to their bodies, advice doulas and other women-focused professionals have been saying for years.

You, and only you, know how you feel at any given moment during pregnancy. And you, and only you, know what's happening inside of your body as you resume your life after birth and add caring for your newborn.

Although it is tempting to want to look different, patience is the key. It took nine months to look nine months pregnant. It will probably take that long to not look it. Of course, issues like adequate nutrition, energy level, and positive living also play a part in a mother's ever changing body. How she takes care of herself postpartum determines more about her body than anything else. And I'm not talking about dieting.

Our society bombards new mothers with constant details about losing pregnancy weight instead of living in healthy ways. You probably already know my feelings about this kind of thinking. I disagree with it and routinely fight against it. Why? My rationale is simple. I have no problem with women feeling the need to look good. My objection stems from the pressure too many new mothers feel to achieve the "perfect" physical image of new motherhood. This way of thinking can lead to dieting and exercise to the extreme in order to push, not guide, the body into postbirth shape.

For many mothers, nothing they do will make them look like their prepregnant self. Their bodies are simply . . . different. Hips seem to have moved and breasts . . . well, I'll leave that discussion until later in this chapter.

For now, whether you are an exercise queen or not, I want you to visualize your body and any thought of exercise as a complete circle of healthy living that keeps you in balance, not necessarily a size 8. You may not be a size 8 again for months, if ever.

Unfortunately, pregnant mothers who are planning for their postpartum selves have no postpartum section in a clothing store to turn to for loose-fitting, body-loving clothes for sore bottoms and changing tops. If you are like most mothers, you will not be able to look at your maternity outfits without wanting to scream. Stay in them, though, for the first couple of weeks and then buy some simple mix and matches in a size comfortable for your fuller body. As the weeks pass, gradually move into clothes that fit your form. This may mean saying good-bye to most of your prepregnancy gear.

If I seem to be hinting that you should let go of your former self, in many ways, I am. You have grown and been altered by becoming a parent. Our fast-paced society neither recognizes nor anticipates the magnitude of the alteration of parenthood. Too many mothers enter into this journey ill prepared for the emotional and the psychological changes and gifts that await them. All birth mothers carry the physical effects of being pregnant and living with a postpregnant body.

Your thoughts about your body can affect your motivation and your willingness to see the beauty of each part of you.

GETTING COMFORTABLE WITH YOUR BODY
The following box contains incomplete sentences that I want you to fill in as you read them. Speak truthfully from your heart about the topics covered here. Giving what you consider the "right" response will not help you uncover the truth of your feelings.

My Body Image
When I look at myself naked, I see someone who looks

_____.

I would compare my breasts to

_____.

I would compare my stomach to

_____.

My bottom and thighs look

_____.

I do these positive things for myself

_____.

My pregnant body was

_____.

I want my body now to look

_____.

Once you have finished the body image exercise, analyze your responses. Note the strength and tone of the words you selected. Did you choose angry, sad, happy, resigned, or factual terms? How did you feel as you were filling in the sentences?

All of these answers point to deep-rooted thoughts about your body that may not be fully formed, even to you.

Exercise

What is exercise? If your concept of physical activity resembles a Tae Bo infomercial, you need to rethink your definition. First, consider this. Have you seen a pregnant woman or a new mother whose breasts are full of milk kicking and pounding in the crowd? No. Why? It's not because there are no women fit enough even after birth to do it. The real reason is no one wants to.

A mother, newly birthed into an individual remotely familiar to the woman she was in the past, has some critical concerns immediately after birth, such as how to urinate with muscles that won't cooperate. And for any mother who has had an episiotomy (an incision in the elastic tissue between the vagina and the anus), a long pushing stage, or even an average labor, every part of her body, and not just her uterus, will be sore, tender, and uncomfortable. This discomfort, especially if it is not alleviated, can persist longer than a few weeks.

Muscles throughout the abdomen, lower back, and diaphragm area may be strained from the exertion of the pushing stage. It is clear that the aftereffects of pushing resonate in the body well past the expulsion of the placenta.

All of these changes for a postpartum mom, not to mention her extra sweat, vaginal secretions, and urine to remove the buildup in the body, mean that her "just gave birth self" doesn't move or feel the same. She may even experience conditions that warrant limiting or omitting exercise entirely.

Balance and Loose Joints.   Stretched ligaments and joints, due to the hormones of pregnancy, may still be loose, making hip and pelvic movements unsteady for a bit. Activities that require balance or coordination may need to wait.

Separated Abdominal Muscles.   Some new mothers have stomach muscles that essentially unzipped to accommodate their growing uterus. You can check for this separation postpartum, medically called diastasis recti, by stretching out on your back on a flat surface. Bend your knees and place one set of fingers pointing toward your feet, just below the center of your rib cage. Take a deep breath and use your other hand to grasp the back of your thigh as you slowly raise your head and shoulders.

Look at the space directly under and to the sides of the fingers near your diaphragm for any indentations. Any sunken gaps are an indication of diastasis recti. If you have this, and many mothers do, your first job will be to knit back and strengthen the muscles before attempting any regular exercise activities.

There are exercises to do this, as well as Velcro belts that can be worn for extra support. Talk to your practitioner about both of these options.

Fatigue.   New mothers, especially after they experience a postbirth hormonal high, are swamped by brain-numbing fatigue. Sleep becomes a necessity that is infrequently encountered by new mothers in most hospital environments. Visitors, family members, bustling employees, and crying babies keep many mothers in a heightened state of awareness of everything that goes on around them. This often translates, upon arrival at home, to sleep depravation. The last thing a sleep-deprived mother needs to do is worry about losing pregnancy weight gain. She has a prescription to sleep whenever her baby is sleeping and to rest to let her body heal. Jumping into exercise too soon could affect more than just her body size. It could adversely affect her health.

A Cesarean Section.   First-time mothers imagine the birth of their babies minus surgery. Unfortunately, unless something drastically changes in the maternity care system in the United States, nearly 22 percent of mothers will have a surgical birth in order to bring their babies into the world. You know from your reading in Chapter 6 that a cesarean is major surgery that requires weeks, maybe even months, to recover from. The last thing a mother who has had a cesarean needs is to consume herself with changing her physical shape. Her body, at this point, is simply trying to ravel itself back together. Stitches need to heal and muscular tissue needs to recover. Exercise can wait.

An Episiotomy.   While having an episiotomy isn't life threatening, it can be uncomfortable as it starts to heal. In terms of its impact on exercise, an episiotomy makes movement difficult by limiting leg, thigh, and deep knee bends.

Of course, it is possible to start exercising once the body has healed a bit without resorting to gyms, machines, or videotapes. Start with your baby. Babies, on average, weigh about seven pounds. A newborn will lose a little of this weight within the first few days before this trend stops.

Carrying a seven- or eight-pound baby, when you are physically able, not only aids the relationship between mother and baby but also gives her a workout. Muscles in a mother's arms are slowly shaped by "baby curling" her baby.

Not interested in curling your baby? Pick up a five-pound sack of sugar or flour instead. This is a convenient way to lift weights.

If you aren't strong enough for something that heavy, settle for cans of fruits or vegetables. These objects are light, easy to grasp, and affordable for under a dollar!

If curling isn't your thing, do housework. The movements of sweeping, vacuuming, mopping, or folding clothes are moves that you might see in stretching, dance, gymnastics, or yoga exercises. Although cleaning isn't very exciting, it can help to restore balance in the body.

Of course, in the first few weeks postpartum, no mother should have to do housework. If I could turn this into a law, I would. No mom should have to stoop or pull anything until she feels ready.

Fortunately, one thing that a mother can and should do for her body that may inadvertently aid in movement and blood circulation is touch, stroke, and cuddle with her partner. Loving massages and light lovemaking can stimulate blood flow and benefit tired tissue. This type of activity should not be done until both partners are ready and willing to be together.

Although I have mentioned free, easy-to-do exercises and activities, there is nothing wrong with attending an exercise class. You should find out if the activity is appropriate for a newly postpartum mom and if the instructor has had any training in postpartum physiology. You want to remain healthy while you are participating in the class or program.

Bringing physical activity into your life should not be limited to regaining your former shape. The act of moving your body should also be for the benefit of your mind and spirit. Exercising solely to achieve a thinner body can lead to an almost disjointed purpose. Instead of exercising to fuel her mothering self with energy and renewed strength, a mother may view exercise as her only chance to reclaim some sense of her former self, the person she used to be. Being active for this reason may cause resentment and even guilt to percolate and become something compulsive since it is not part of a long-term plan for healthy living.

Being a mother is a wonderful gift. Being a healthy mother is a necessity in order to parent from a well of positive energy and evolve into a being who is simultaneously called mother, wife, lover, sister, daughter, and friend. Balancing all of these roles can force even a mother with a strong sense of self to question her sanity.

It's not the idea of exercise that can cause this, but the determination to lose weight at any cost: including time with baby and nutritional needs.

Body Fuel

You have heard plenty about nutrition during pregnancy, including discussion in this book about food from a simple, healthy living perspective. This idea continues, unchanged, into the postpartum period.

New mothers need fuel for their bodies to adequately bounce back from birth and to care for their babies. A mother's body after birth, pushed to the edge and back, takes weeks to rebound from the total exhaustion of bringing a new baby into the world. Add to this need the role of caring for a new baby and you have a recipe for fatigue.

The first way to combat the fatigue of postpartum is to set yourself up with support people who can help you care for your newborn as you sleep and eat to regain your strength. Postpartum doulas give new mothers the kind of one-on-one attention and special care that women in a variety of cultures around the world already receive. Amazingly, many of these cultural practices involve a mother resting for a set period of weeks or days, drinking hot drinks, avoiding cold air, and being attended to by the women in her community or in her family. A postpartum doula is in many cases a surrogate "sister friend," a woman ready to pass on knowledge and support, mothering a new mother into her self.

Other than finding and obtaining this vital person, a new mother should also arrange the people in her life like a cozy shawl. Look at your own friends and family. Each person who is important to you can and should take over running the house and caring for you and your baby in the first weeks postpartum. Resting, even when you are too tired to sleep, will aid your overworked body to unwind and de-stress.

Yet, perhaps the most essential way for a mother to stave off mind-numbing fatigue is with excellent nutrition. New mothers are encouraged to consume plenty of protein, calcium, iron, and nutrient-rich fruits and vegetables. Generally, postpartum mothers do not need to follow a special diet. A mother's main goal is to provide herself with as many opportunities as possible to consume healthy foods.

Eat When Hungry.   Never skip meals in an attempt to lose weight or because of fatigue. (This is a common motherhood ailment.) If you are too tired to prepare a meal for yourself, get someone to do it for you. You only make it harder for your body to realign itself after birth if you start skipping meals. You can also force yourself, by skipping mealtimes, to reach for anything to make the hunger pains go away. A candy bar looks like a tempting lunch when you are desperate for a sugar boost. It's only afterward that the burst of energy turns into sugar depression.

Need further convincing of the benefits of eating well? The Stockholm Pregnancy and Weight Development Study to identify risk factors for postpartum weight issues such as dietary habits and activity found that mothers are more likely to return to their prepregnancy size when they eat regular meals that include a balanced breakfast and lunch.

Keep It Simple.   It is possible to experience temporary constipation after birth. This discomfort is caused by a variety of sources that collectively slow down bowel movements. Muscles in a mother's anus are stretched, and pregnancy hormones have further relaxed tissue throughout the digestive tract so that the bowels move in a pattern slower than normal.

Keeping your diet consistent with your normal food choices, as well as temporarily avoiding things that can increase indigestion and stomach irregularities, will help you reduce the chances of experiencing any problems at all.

Over time, increase your flavors and spices gradually until you feel that your body is ready to digest anything you want to give it.

Keep Food and Drinks Handy. Ask any new mother what she would do if she became thirsty just after her baby settled down to nurse. Odds are she would say that her needs at that moment wouldn't matter. You too may get in the habit of providing for your baby before yourself. (A behavior that I will show later in this chapter is biologically driven.) But putting off fluid because you are too busy to drink will turn you into a dehydrated mother who produces less milk.

To adequately care for your baby and stave off any postbirth complications brought on by inadequate rest and nutrition—like anemia—set up a few food areas in your home. These "food centers" should be scattered throughout your home, and within reach of each of your baby centers.

Place water in ready-to-drink containers and deposit quick snacks like nuts, raisins, dried fruits, grapes, or bananas in each of your food centers. This will allow you easy access to quality snacks that are easy to eat and full of much needed nutrients. Caring for a baby is guaranteed to force a mother to use every square inch of her home to store or care for her baby.

Unfortunately, eating at food centers in your home won't work once you leave it for your first walk with your newborn. What should you do then? Eat on the run? For most moms, that's exactly what they do. For the sake of your health, avoid fast food if you can. Fast food reminds you quickly why it's made fast. Other options exist but may not be the best choice in the early days.

Stopping at a café or diner will be more like a day visit, since it seems to take hours to eat and then leave after feeding baby and yourself, changing diapers, and then packing up your baby supplies, stroller, carrier, diaper bag, purse, and so on.

Make your life easier by packing light food items for your day trips out. Place cut fruit and vegetables, crackers, cheeses, and other delicious foods in small Ziploc bags. Pick items that can be eaten with one hand. This will be your main mode of feeding yourself for a number of months; get used to it.

Try to avoid chocolate, alcohol, and caffeine. While postpartum hormonal changes may be mentally and emotionally challenging, they can be physically demanding as the body responds biochemically to certain food stimuli. Chocolate, caffeine, and alcohol can make you feel moody, irritable, spacey, and hyperactive before altering your emotions once again after the effects have worn off.

Although you may not sense the changes in your body after consuming these things, your baby will. Each of these items will stay in your bloodstream for hours. Most important, though, they can enter a delicate newborn's food source—mother's breast-milk—and temporarily alter his body chemistry.

WATER

Follow your pregnancy routine and try to consume two and a half quarts of water a day. Use a cleaned, recycled plastic or glass container for your water. If you consume your two and a half quarts of water and are still thirsty, just drink more.

You can also have juices, milk, and other decaffeinated drinks. Watch out for tea, coffee, and sodas since they can dehydrate you.

You, and only you, can find a healthy balance for your life. By focusing on your physical core and conceiving of it as a part of yourself that has to be healthy, you are priming your body to move from pregnancy through birth and into the role of motherhood with strength.

As you probably already surmised, motherhood is an amazing job that is anxiety provoking, fear inducing, and heart-grippingly intense. There is no magic formula or chant I can give you that will make the experience any less intense. However, there are things you can do for yourself and your family that allow the journey to be undertaken with heart, courage, and positive belief in your ability to raise a child.

Start this strength building by following the hints and suggestions in these pages about your physical body. Knowing what's happening in the middle part of your body will help you handle the obvious and mysterious physical alterations at the top and bottom of your torso. The top, your breasts, receives a lot of attention before pregnancy, but scant focus during and after birth. However, the bottom of your torso—your vagina, perineum, and anus—is ignored entirely.

DISCOVERING WHAT'S GOING ON
AROUND YOUR BOTTOM

The main action of birth occurs in and around the vagina. It is here that parents get their first real glimpse of their baby during a vaginal birth. However, other major changes also occur in this area after birth. The three main parts, a mother's vagina, perineum, and anus, go through substantial alterations as tissue expands, contracts, and adapts to the rise and fall of a new mother's hormones. Mothers today need to be prepared for these changes and to be aware of ways to lessen discomforts.

Brace yourself for this discussion. No topic is left unturned. You will find a frank discussion of vaginal dryness, contraception, orgasms, incontinence, sitz baths, hemorrhoids, and lubrication jelly. If you are embarrassed reading about what you consider intimate issues, don't be. Embarrassment holds no place in a discussion about your health and well-being.

This section focuses on arming you with self-care suggestions and advice in order for you to understand and live in your body holistically. For medical advice about particular problems, contact your doctor or midwife. A number of professional organizations and resources are included in these pages.

The first area we will examine is often ignored and routinely misunderstood: the vagina.

The Vagina

For centuries, women have fought a long battle over their private parts. Well before the first wave of feminists were born, issues of women's sexuality confounded both men and women. Scholars have, over the years, written about women's supposed instability, erratic tendencies, and general hysteria due to the condition of their uterus, ovaries, and vagina. Somehow, some way, the power of a woman's sex, and her ability to produce a child, made her body parts half mythical and half sacred.

Look around the world. Of the cultures that have a high reverence for the power of a woman's body, pregnancy and birth are considered major moments of spiritual attainment. A mother taps into some feminine source of energy that connects her to the women who have given birth throughout time, and the females yet to come. Her status as a mother is elevated beyond that of a mere person; she is a mother, a bearer of human life.

Aisha Qandisha, a Moroccan goddess, Anahita, a Persian goddess, and Ishtar, an Assyrian goddess, were embodiments of fertility and sexuality during a time in history when a woman's body was not hidden and ignored. These mythical female goddesses merged femininity, fertility, and sexuality into one being—something that you too are attempting to do, no matter how you define these terms. Belief in the goddess is alive and well throughout the world. Regardless of the religious overtones of goddess worship, the concepts and images provide positive portraits of women's sexuality and procreative powers.

A glance at our society shows a culture determined to silence the mystery and the wonder of a woman's body while also objectifying some ideal of female beauty. These opposing, often conflicting ideas create an atmosphere of confusion for women, especially during and after childbirth.

The area intimately involved in birthing a baby is the same area that women powder, douche, and spray to smell and appear like something other than what it is: a fertile, rich environment designed to do magical things.

If you find this concept hard to believe, you are not alone. Many women understand that babies grow in their wombs and then come out of their vaginas. They just cannot see the power and the strength of that act.

Understandably, a number of women's health professionals and scholars believe that the power of a woman's body is subverted by the technology-driven maternity system in the United States. They contend that the sheer rise in cesareans and episiotomies sends a message to women that there is something inherently wrong with their bodies, and they need technology to fix it. These vocal opponents of technology-driven maternity care feel that women are not the center of care; technology resides in that spot.

Naomi Wolf, in her book *Misconceptions*, describes this scene from her labor: "The fetal monitor . . . became the center of activity . . . the baby and I seemed less real . . . than did the machine" (137). This sense of powerlessness adds to the conflicting dilemma of femininity, sexuality, and maternity.

A new mother, looking at her changing genitalia, has to work hard to visualize herself being sexual and maternal at the same time. The ideas on this topic within our culture suggest to mothers that their genitalia are neutral.

Take a moment to ponder this: a few years ago, an actress, Lisa Rinna, posed in a pictorial in *Playboy* magazine. The caption under her name on the cover said, "Proud, Pregnant, and Beautiful." Some in the media responded to this event with confusion. The dilemma stemmed not from questioning why a woman would want to be photographed in various states of undress, but why a pregnant woman thought anyone would want to see her naked form. The implication was that she was too fat and unbecoming to be seen.

It's amazing that centuries after pregnant, upper-middle-class women confined themselves to their homes because of their "unseemly" looks, we have not moved much farther in our acceptance and recognition of the courage and strength of motherhood.

Of course, many women don't feel beautiful and strong during pregnancy or the months after birth. The demands of a new baby and the healing processes of their evolving form overwhelm any chance to find pleasure in their bodies. It may take months or years before they start to recognize a woman under all that baby gear. However, she is there, from top to bottom.

Consider the vagina, for a moment. This sheath-like cavity extends from the opening between the legs to surround the cervix. The vagina is located behind a mother's bladder and is in front of her rectum.

While many mothers have put a tampon inside their vagina, few know exactly what it feels like inside. According to Dr. Pepper Schwartz, a prominent sex scholar, about 20 percent of women have masturbated at some point in their lives. Because it is possible to investigate one's body without trying to achieve orgasm, more women should check out this part of their body. They will find that their vagina is surrounded on the outside by tissue that engorges and fills with blood during arousal. Called the labia majora and minora, these folds protect the sensitive tissue that is at the opening of the vagina and the hooded clitoris, the female analogue to the penis.

Inside the vagina are mucous membranes that release vaginal fluid throughout a woman's menstrual cycle, during pregnancy, after birth, and in large amounts during arousal. The mucous membranes are covered with ridges, or cone-like indentations that actually fan out or expand to accommodate a lover's penis or a baby head. It is about seven and a half centimeters in length on one side, and nine centimeters (that extends behind the cervix) on the other.

Enlarged by the baby after birth and tender in many spots, the vagina slowly tightens its loosened muscular tone while being bathed in lochia. The lochia, part of the fluid released by the uterus, actually goes through stages in its coloration. The initial darker red tone that comes out in the first few days and weeks postpartum is replaced by a lighter, pinker color as the blood volume decreases. Intermittent spotting characterizes the last few weeks of lochia flow until the bleeding ceases, signaling the return of the uterus to prepregnancy size.

This blood flow might cause the sensitive skin that surrounds the vagina to be caked in dried blood. You can lessen this discomfort by rinsing the outer folds of the vagina periodically with warm water. Pat the area dry.

While you are noting your lochia flow, pay attention to your ability to pass urine. Your urethra, perched just behind the clitoris and in front of the vagina, has also been altered by the birth of the baby. A tube about four centimeters long, the urethra contains muscular and mucous tissue that is highly reactive to pregnancy and birth. Its alterations after birth can possibly cause urinary incontinence.

Incontinence refers to the unfortunate circumstance of leaking urine. In many instances, incontinence is mild and is only apparent late in pregnancy, because of the pressure of the baby on the bladder, and just after birth, due to the distention of the urethra and other connective tissue near the vagina. Postbirth, this typically means that a mother cannot stop or start urine flow easily. This may mean that you will need to run water in the sink to trigger the urge to urinate. The nerves inside the urethra, essentially desensitized by birth, may take a few days to remember how to work.

Be patient with this. Your body will return to its normal functioning. If you would like to increase your muscle tone in both your vaginal and urethral tissues, do Kegel exercises.

Kegel exercises involve tightening the entire perineal area in increments, as if you are going up in an elevator, until you cannot tighten them anymore. Once you reach the highest level you can achieve, hold that position for four or five beats. As the early days of postpartum turn into weeks, practice Kegels whenever you find yourself sitting. These exercises for your vagina are strengthening and toning calisthenics that can help your vaginal muscles emerge from birth stronger than before you were pregnant.

After you have practiced Kegels for a number of weeks, try to stop your urine flow in midstream and then resume. This takes considerable muscle control and can signal return of coordination.

For a real educational exercise, when your area is no longer ultratender or swollen, have your partner insert his finger into your vagina. (Trust me: This is an educational exercise!) Make sure his hands are clean and his nails are trimmed. Try, with his finger inside your vagina, to grasp his finger tightly with your vaginal muscles. This exercise is a way to intimately examine your vagina with your partner to determine whether your baby's birth canal is ready to return to its other role: an erogenous zone.

Amorous feelings, or even thoughts, may be months in coming. This temporary decrease in sexuality is normal for many women. Initially, the body needs to heal. Prolonged lack of desire or intimacy that lasts consistently for months on end is concerning. Intimacy, though, is not just about sex. Intimacy points to a very deep or close connection or union between two people. Sex is only one part of intimacy. It is essentially the physical representation of feelings of desire, love, and need with a partner (not necessarily in that order). There are many ways to experience intimacy.

New mothers are primarily concerned with their rate of sexual relations with their partners, and how their bodies appear to them. Some fear that their partners might no longer desire them since they have lost some of their zest after having their babies. These and other "ideas" about intimacy and sex postpartum are told and retold to every mother by well-meaning friends who have no evidence to support their "truths."

It's my goal to debunk many of the myths of sex and intimacy that pervade the minds of new mothers, making them more agitated and stressed about their relationship with their partner and their view of their body. I offer this information to answer questions you may be pondering or fears you may be harboring about sex, intimacy, and what other women are experiencing.

There are hundreds of myths about sex, sexuality, and women and men's bodies. For our purposes, I will focus on nine of the most prominent. Each myth presented here is correlated to a seminal article that appeared in the *Journal of Psychosomatic Research*. This meta-analysis, conducted by Dr. Kirsten von Sydow, examined fifty-nine studies from 1950 to 1996, offering the most comprehensive overview of sexuality, pregnancy, and motherhood. Combining psychological and medical studies, Sydow describes the first systematic analysis of what men and women are really thinking and doing about sex during pregnancy and after birth.

It is, without a doubt, the best overall presentation of sex and motherhood that I have found. With its help, I will illuminate what is really happening sexually with a new mother.

NINE SEXUAL MYTHS

Myth 1: Most couples have sex within the first month after childbirth

Contrary to assumptions, most couples wait six to eight weeks before resuming intercourse. Part of this delay stems from the overall fatigue of a mother's body and her need to recover from birth.

When a mother's genitalia is no longer tender or swollen, the thought of intimacy might appear in her mind one day, but it has to battle the fatigue of caring for a newborn infant. Sometimes it is difficult for a new mother to reconcile her various roles into one strong being and figure out how to do everything that she wants without being smothered in the process.

Even waiting six to eight weeks does not guarantee that a mother enjoys intercourse. Sydow found that only 20 percent of new mothers have an orgasm during their first intercourse postbirth.

Time, though, is not the greatest indicator of readiness. Amorous feelings and physical need are more potent signs of your readiness for intimacy with your partner.

Myth 2: Most women resume their sexual interest and activity at levels they had before pregnancy within weeks or maybe a few months of giving birth

Sydow was able to demonstrate that many women experience sexual problems after giving birth. This could include vaginal dryness, painful or difficult intercourse, or loss of desire. And this experience can even translate to avoidance. Sydow found that of the women experiencing problems during intercourse, 64 percent will go on to steer clear of having intercourse entirely. Called dyspareunia, pain during intercourse may be the result of something simple, like a healing episiotomy scar, or it may indicate something that should be discussed with a health professional.

A 1999 article in the *Archives of Sexual Behavior* found that only 19 percent of women in the study discussed their postnatal sexual problems with a professional. The lesson for any new mother is to discuss any concern she may have with someone. That is the surest way to have any difficulties observed and even medically managed.

Myth 3: Partners want sex soon after the birth of their child

There is a lack of concrete data focused primarily on fathers and their sexual feelings and activities before, during, and after the birth of their babies. Even without evidence, women continue to be concerned enough about satisfying their partners sexually that they engage in sexual activity even while still experiencing pain, discomfort, and anxiety about sexual relations because they are certain their partners need it.

Little is understood about fathers and their desire and need for sex after the birth of their babies. Interestingly, one study observed by Sydow found that fathers actually were less interested in sex after they had their first child. The cause was unknown, but it illuminates the confusion and possibly conflicting thoughts and ideas that affect fathers as well.

One way researchers learn what fathers and mothers are thinking about each other is to ask them. Whether this is a poor survey question or parents are reluctant to discuss intimate matters on questionnaires or with strangers, the outcome is still the same: Little is said or asked in current research studies about postnatal communication between partners. Communication is the only way that each person within a relationship knows what the other is thinking and feeling. If a mother is uncomfortable discussing these issues with a partner, someone—a friend, counselor, practitioner, or doula—can provide a sounding board for concerns.

Myth 4: Women prefer not to be touched at all after childbirth

Although it is clear that fathers are the ones to initiate sex after birth with mothers, women are far from withdrawn.

Sydow found the following preferences among women in terms of stimulation and activity after birth:

41–53 percent   prefer nongenital tenderness
25–32 percent   prefer clitoral stimulation
23–30 percent   prefer breast stimulation
15–30 percent   prefer vaginal stimulation
 6–16 percent   prefer oral stimulation by their partner
 4–11 percent   prefer to give oral stimulation to their partner

Myth 5: Intercourse occurs too often for a new mother and not often enough for her partner

This idea is perpetuated in assumptions about fathers' sexual interests and needs. As already mentioned, little is known about their feelings and needs; unfortunately, much is made up. What is not made up is the fact that frequency of intercourse can signal problems.

Distractions, disinterest, and even disease can strain a couple's intimacy. Studies suggest that frequency of intercourse decreases during the first year postpartum before eventually, two years later, occurring 1–2 times a week.

This is not abnormal unless it is a sharp decrease in the "normal" rate for a couple. How often you and your partner are together is the rate based on your needs and desires as a couple, not the rate reported as the average in a study.

Myth 6: Talking to someone about sexuality after childbirth cannot really alleviate problems

This nugget is so immensely false that I have to include it. Far too often, new mothers convince themselves that talking to someone, reading, or informing themselves of sexual issues won't make their concerns go away. This couldn't be further from the truth.

Studies show that receiving advice about sex from books (such as this), birth preparation classes, or friends increases a mother's enjoyment of or interest in sex.

If you find yourself needing more technical advice or information, reach out to the American Association of Sex Educators, Counselors, and Therapists (AASECT). This organization, founded in 1967, strives to educate and certify professionals who engage in sex education, counseling, and therapy. They maintain a database of certified professionals across the country available for support. Their Web address is www.aasect.org.

If you only want information, seek out the Sexuality Information and Education Council of the United States (SIECUS). Founded around the same time as AASECT, this organization is dedicated to promoting sexuality education for people of all ages. Although well-known for sex education in schools, SIECUS also provides other support, including the Mary S. Calderone Library, claimed to be the most comprehensive library of all aspects of human sexuality in the world. SIECUS is found at www.siecus.org.

Both of these organizations, and others like them, are excellent sources of information that can be, in many cases, accessed directly from your own home.

Professionals involved in sexuality education and counseling strive to make couples and individuals feel comfortable, supported, and helped with whatever concerns or problems they are seeking to remedy.

For simple ideas about spicing up intimacy, look to the World Wide Web for a myriad of sites geared toward women and couples. Be prepared, though, to find everything you ever thought or has been thought about sex. The Web is truly the last great frontier. You can simplify your search by following SIECUS and AASECT's Web site links to quality sex information on the Web.

Myth 7: Episiotomies, forceps, suction delivery, or prolonged second stage has no effect on a mother's sexual enjoyment or start of sexual activity

Although more studies need to be done, current data suggests a correlation between painful intercourse and perineal laceration, including episiotomy, a procedure often done in conjunction with forceps delivery and vacuum extraction.

An April 2001 study by Signorello et al. in the *American Journal of Obstetrics and Gynecology* found that women with second-degree trauma to their perineal tissue were 80 percent more likely to experience painful intercourse at three months postpartum, whereas mothers with third- and fourth-degree trauma (considered the worst) were 270 percent more likely to feel pain or discomfort during intercourse.

Whether desired or not, intervention remains a reality for many mothers. The aftereffects of some obstetrical interventions can last for months.

What you can do for your body is learn ways to aid its recovery without doing things that inadvertently extend discomfort. Not wearing restrictive clothing, like tight underwear, is one of the simple things you can do to help your body heal.

Myth 8: If a mother's partner is anxious and wants sex, she should be with him out of wifely duty or obligation

Sexuality is a healthy part of a person's life that should be enjoyed. My mantra about sex and intimacy is the same for a new mother as it is for a pregnant one: Don't be intimate if you feel pain or discomfort, or if you lack desire. Each one of those things indicates that help or more time to heal is needed before sex can resume.

The last thing a fatigue-ridden, sleep-deprived new mother needs is something else to do. Engaging in sexual relations out of a sense of duty makes it a chore or a service, not an enjoyable moment spent with a loved one. Sex, though, has many benefits, for example, releasing tension and increasing blood flow to tissue.

Positively embracing sex in the early months postpartum may be extremely difficult for you to do. Research shows that mental and emotional concerns and instability postpartum are real for many mothers. These issues do not just affect a mother's ability to care for her baby and identify herself as a new mother; they also impact her sexually. How often you have sex, your enjoyment of it, and even your romantic feelings about your partner are rolled up in these issues.

You have heard that the most powerful sexual organ is the mind. The brain and its workings reach into every corner of a new mother's life. If she experiences instability, anxiety, or stress, she may become trapped in a vicious loop of disarray where nothing is as it should be. These issues, left untreated or unresolved, can cause many problems. This is one big reason why a new mother's mental and spiritual cores are essential parts to strengthen and renew.

Myth 9: Positive sexuality is a nice goal, but it doesn't really have an impact on a couple's relationship

Sydow observed that increased sexual activity and enjoyment is correlated to a positive healthy image; furthermore, the quality of a couple's relationship is also based on positive sexual ideas and enjoyment. This is not just a short-term benefit. A 1988 study found that three years after the birth of a baby, a couple's relationship is "more stable" the more sexual a couple has remained.

This evidence should not push you to have sex with your partner every day in the hopes that sex will keep divorce away. What has to happen in your life is a more realistic and individualistic approach to sexual satisfaction.

The intimate and sexual relationship that you maintain and develop with your partner has to be based on the reality of your relationship and your changing needs now that both of you are parents as well as partners.

For some parents, trying to be parents and partners can cause problems. Thankfully, there are ways to head many problems off before they become major disruptions.

Troubleshooting

These nine myths of sexuality bring up many of the issues that doulas discuss with new mothers during their postpartum visits.

This topic penetrates many of the personal issues of motherhood and sexuality that new mothers have to grapple with. Equally prominent are concerns about ways to maintain the health and strength of the body.

The myths just discussed contain numerous suggestions for enriching and enlivening your intimate relationship with your partner. However, these are just the tip of the iceberg. There are many things you can do to have a healthy sex life as a new mother.

Build up intimacy slowly. Each week after the birth of your baby, engage in an intimate act with your partner. For the first week, make it hugging or combing each other's hair. Your tender parts probably won't want much more.

Within a month postpartum, branch out to massages. Both of you will probably need it. By week five and six, you could be ready for kissing and touching that you may or may not want to lead to orgasm. Sometime within this next month is the best time to see how both of you feel about sexual intercourse.

If you are ready, start by doing simple things. Turn off the TV. Familiarize yourselves with the smell and feel of each other. Hopefully, your tenderness and stroking throughout the previous weeks has enabled the moment to be marked with less anxiety and performance pressure than if the two of you weren't already adding layers of intimacy to your relationship. Come prepared for this moment with cloths for any leaking milk and lubrication for vaginal dryness, especially if you are still breastfeeding. You should also anticipate the need for extended, gentle foreplay for both of you.

Because of stress and hormonal changes, it may take longer to reach orgasm. Any sexual release may feel different from what you experienced before you were pregnant, if you have it at all. This, of course, is one of the biggest issues new mothers confront during their first intimate moment with their partner: they struggle with the pressure to make sex better than before they gave birth. If you expect explosions and flashing lights in orgasmic ecstasy, you may be unprepared for only a little sizzle.

The first time may not be the best, but think of it as the ball that will get everything rolling again.

If you aren't ready, talk about this to your partner and keep the communication flowing. An honest, open relationship in which you talk about these issues can help you alleviate troubles before they become larger problems.

TALKING ABOUT CONTRACEPTION

As difficult as it might be to imagine, a new mother can become pregnant again within a month after giving birth. This little practical joke is not funny to the women who have gone on to have two babies less than a year apart.

Years ago, I had a colleague who had twins after months of fertility treatments. She did not breast-feed her sons and ignored contraception, given the type of medical assistance she needed to conceive her twins in the first place. Imagine her shock after her twins' first month of life to find herself pregnant again. This mother suddenly had three children nine months later.

This mother dearly loves her children. Yet she wishes she could have spaced them out for both her mental and physical health.

Becoming pregnant again within weeks of giving birth is probably not in your game plan. Not being a mother again in a matter of months will only happen if you get real about the chance of making a baby each time you have sex with your partner. Discuss contraception with your partner today.

Because you can ovulate before your first menstrual flow, waiting until after your first period is literally after the egg has already come. That's too late to prevent anything other than another pregnancy.

What options do you have? The most common choices for new mothers are condoms, birth control pills, and other devices. Breast-feeding moms need to select a contraception option that will not disrupt their milk supply with hormones. All moms, though, should forego contraception that resides inside their vaginas, against their cervixes, or inside their uteruses. The evolving shape of a postpartum mom's perineal area means that what fits today is sure not to fit tomorrow. Plus, the risk of infection is high with devices like an IUD at this time.

You can also practice a method known as natural family planning. If you choose to follow your mucous secretions and ovulation signs, be serious about it and read up on this approach to natural birth control.

YOUR PERINEUM AND ANUS

The perineum is an area of superficial and deep muscular tissue, fibers, nerves, and vessels that actually include the points above and around the clitoris, all the way back to the anus. Full of vessels and fibers that are involved in urine flow, sex, bowel movements, and birth, the perineum is an essential part of a woman's body to keep healthy throughout her life cycle.

Kegel exercises are one way to tone the perineum, but there are other things that can be done to help heal this tender part of a woman's body.

Witch hazel. This plant extract product relieves swelling and aids circulation around any sensitive stitches between a mother's vagina and anus, and any swollen tissue that needs relief.

An easy and beneficial doula tip: Soak small gauze pads in witch hazel and then place them in small plastic bags for freezing. Put the frozen gauze pads on your menstrual or obstetrical pads worn to collect lochia. The cold will aid swelling and circulation and the witch hazel will soothe the area.

Sitz baths. These are small tubs that you can sit in periodically during the day. The healing warm water soothes an aching perineum. You can acquire a sitz bath at your local pharmacy. Most sitz baths can conveniently fit over the bowl of a toilet for quick and easy sitting.

Rubber rings. Because prolonged sitting when nursing and caring for your baby can feel uncomfortable, obtain a rubber ring (also available at most pharmacies) to sit on. Purchase a couple for your home and one for your car so that you can be comfortable everywhere. Some rings can be filled with warm water for even greater enjoyment.

Perineal cleansing. Acidic urine can burn a swollen, achy episiotomy wound and irritate sensitive flesh. Rubbing the area during a regular bathroom visit can only serve to bring more discomfort.

Lower your chances of experiencing more pain by cleaning your entire perineum with warm water sprayed from a handy bottle you can keep in the bathroom.

As soon as you sit on the toilet, fill the plastic bottle with warm water that you spray on yourself after you are done. Lightly pat your skin dry with toilet paper, change pads, put a new drop of witch hazel on it, and you will be ready to tackle the world again.

Time. Episiotomies feel worse before they get better. Some practitioners think episiotomies are routine, simple procedures. Other women's health professionals consider episiotomy an intervention that occasionally aids in birth outcomes, while causing immense physical discomfort postpartum. This is due to the linear incision and subsequent tight stitches placed in the blood-rich area of the perineum. A mother who needs to heal from an episiotomy should give herself time to recover from all that her body has been through.

Water, balanced diet, moving around. As simple as it sounds, drinking water, eating a healthy diet, and walking around can move blood and digested foodstuff through a mother's body, ensuring that she remains regular, healthy, and able to produce any needed repairs to her body. Keeping one-self healthy and fit can often do more to bring about satisfactory mothering than reading all the books on parenting.

As you can imagine, the lower part of your torso, your genitals, are affected in different ways after your baby's birth. For the continued health and vitality of all your tender parts, nurture your body as well as your baby. Your body, the "thing" that will stay with you for your life cycle, can emerge from birth and carry you through motherhood healthy and strong, but only if you take steps to stay in tune with your body's adjustments and needs. This, of course, includes the many changes that happen to your breasts. Whether you choose to breast-feed or not, your body starts the preparations to feed your baby nature's perfectly made baby food.

DISCOVERING WHAT'S HAPPENING
TO YOUR BREASTS

No one can convince me that food made by a mother's own body is second best for her baby. This isn't political bickering or self-righteous doula muttering, but scientific fact.

A mother's breast milk adapts to her baby's needs. Consider this: Studies have found that the milk made by mothers of preterm babies contains extra salt, nitrogen, protein, and sugar in order for their undergrown babies to develop faster. Every mother's breast milk changes during a feeding, providing milk (called foremilk) that is high in protein, low in fat and calories, followed by milk (hind milk) that is high in fat, calories, and protein. Foremilk looks watery while hind milk appears thick and creamy.

But breast milk offers more than just its nutritional content. More and more studies suggest that breast-fed babies are healthier, suffer from fewer allergies, have potentially higher IQs, and seem less likely to be affected by SIDS. However, breast-feeding is what happens after birth. Changes occur to the breasts during pregnancy that prepares mammary tissue for feeding.

Cauliflower-like clusters within the breast enlarge and prepare to make and secrete breast milk. Channels that will move the milk down near the areola and the nipple get primed for this job. But perhaps the greatest change is hormonal. Hormones involved in breast-feeding increase slowly during the last weeks of pregnancy until the moment the placenta is pushed out when a flood of breast milk–making hormones erupt in a mother's body.

Breasts respond to all of these changes from the onset of pregnancy by growing in size. The size of a mother's breasts before pregnancy is immaterial. A-cup or D-cup means nothing to mammary tissue. The clusters grow and become ready for breast-feeding in the same way for every mother. Nipples, though, are another concern since inverted or flat nipples can impede the grasping required of a newborn baby. Talk to your postpartum doula or a lactation consultant about ways that you can limit any problems. Rest assured. Some interesting studies show that babies can adapt to any shape nipple for breast-feeding without fancy shields covering the nipple to pull it out.

For many mothers, the growth of their breasts is shocking. Part of the shock stems from the fact that they rarely see what postpartum breasts are supposed to look like. Our society's fascination with breasts does not extend to nursing or postpartum mothers. Those images are not in the culture for mothers to see and witness. Instead, any interested new mother has to go to a special breast-feeding class or group to find images of what her breasts will become.

Throughout the world, there are societies that have large and small sculptures of pregnant and nursing women showing how fecund and powerful they are with swollen, milk-producing breasts. This image could be you.

Enlarged the first week after birth, your mammary tissue will eventually settle down into its own rhythm once milk is being made on a regular basis. The breasts will be immensely heavy and full during this interval. Applying hot compresses can help with the circulation, and applying frozen washcloths can help with the swelling. Wear a good maternity bra with support in the first few weeks postpartum, even at night. Some companies make special breastfeeding sleep bras that are less restrictive.

This is important since extra blood flows into the entire area. But your breasts are more than just full; they are also working. In the last weeks or months of pregnancy, colostrum develops. Colostrum is a sticky substance that is mineral rich and antibody packed just for a baby. For the health of her newborn, every mother should feed her baby colostrum.

The first day or two after birth, both mother and baby may be tired and want to sleep for stretches at a time. Soon, perhaps within the first hour of life, a mother's baby will latch on to her breast and take in her colostrum. Colostrum is not only packed full of disease-fighting cells for the baby but also contains a laxative-like substance that helps the baby expel the buildup of meconium that has settled in her bottom. Meconium is a tarlike waste product that the baby has made throughout the pregnancy. It usually passes three to five days after birth—the time it usually takes for a mother's milk to be made in the glands in her breasts. As simple as it sounds, breast-feeding is some-

177

thing a number of moms can't imagine themselves doing; others experience frustration as they navigate how to get it done. These mothers turn to soy or cow's milk–based formula because they feel that it is convenient and safe.

Although the convenience and safety of formulas are debated heavily, one thing is clear: From the American Academy of Pediatrics recommendation that mothers breast-feed for at least a year to the Baby Friendly designation of breast-feeding friendly hospitals, breast-feeding is being talked about again. As a doula, I applaud this newfound interest in nature's perfect food. However, I am concerned that some mothers have translated this new interest to mean that they should be able to breast-feed without any help, support, or guidance. Studies are clear that mothers breast-feed longer and with significantly fewer problems if they have continuous and clear support from their partners and their practitioners. Mothers need to feel that breast-feeding is not only something doable but something they can and will learn how to do with their baby.

Some partners are unsure how they feel about their partners nursing until the first breast-feeding session occurs. Suddenly, they may feel uncomfortable seeing what they have perceived as their sexual objects morphing into their babies' meal makers.

If your partner is unsure how to respond to your breast-feeding interest, talk to him at length about how it feels and what you are doing for your baby. Although he needs to understand why your choice is so beneficial, never ignore his uncertainty or belittle his concern. If needed, give him books like this one or *The Womanly Art of Breastfeeding*, by La Leche League International, to help educate him about the immense benefits and purpose of breast-feeding. It may take him a while to separate his amorous thoughts about your breasts from their practical function, but it will eventually happen.

Your partner's support is vital to your continued breast-feeding, but you also need the support of your doctor or midwife, and your baby's pediatrician.

Trying to find practitioners who support breast-feeding mothers has become easier given the interest in nursing and the plethora of studies that have become available over the years. As more media attention is focused on the reality of nursing and the benefits, more mothers learn how amazing the whole process is. But there are still medical professionals who are not as aware of the beauty and the importance of breast-feeding as they should be.

If you encounter a health professional who does not support you 100 percent in this endeavor, exercise your consumer right and search for someone who will. Do not settle for care and service that is not respectful or family-centered.

All of these concerns, though, will seem like a faraway dream the first time you feed your baby.

A baby cries or makes hungry noises when she is ready to eat. Bring her to your nipple. Adjust her body so she does not have to turn or move her head in order to grasp the nipple into her mouth.

She should have her mouth open wide when you "latch" her on in order for her to grab the nipple and about half of the areola into her mouth. Quick suckling leads to oxytocin release in you and something called "letdown" that involves the pumping of milk toward the nipple and baby's waiting mouth.

Because your nipple is deep within her mouth, your milk will be able to easily hit the back of her throat. Her sucking will slow down once milk is filling her belly. Once she has swallowed enough food to stave off her hunger, she will stop sucking and typically fall asleep.

This process sounds like it should be simple, and biologically it is. However, things can happen that can make the process muddled. And once confusion, panic, or misinformation set in, breast-feeding can become frustrating.

From the first latch on by her baby, a mother needs a support team that does not yell, shout, or demand anything. This group roots for a mom and provides as much information as requested so that a mother's breast-feeding goal is met.

What Is Your Breast-Feeding Goal for Your Baby?

1. How long do you want to provide your breast milk to your baby?
2. Are you concerned about how nursing will affect your breasts?
3. Is your partner supportive of breast-feeding?
4. Will you need to go back to work soon after your baby's birth? Will you continue nursing?
5. What is your greatest fear and concern about nursing?
6. What is the greatest benefit that you can see in providing your breast milk to your baby?

Once you have your answers to these questions, notice any trends. Do you seem fearful of body changes or the mechanics of nursing? Which question do you feel has the most impact on the length of time you would like to nurse?

Rest assured, though. You are not the only mother facing breast-feeding questions. Across the country, mothers are grappling with issues big and small about providing their breast milk for their babies. Thankfully, support people and health professionals exist from coast to coast to help any mother they can. Unfortunately, mothers in this country face a society that does not clearly champion the cause of breast-feeding or, some believe, parenting.

Our country still does not guarantee uniform parental leave (even for a small portion of time) for every worker. This can translate into a delayed connection between fathers and their babies because they must assume work responsibilities soon after birth.

This issue can even affect mothers who have to figure out how to combine breast-feeding and working. While there are challenges to working and nursing, you can do it.

Pumping and storing breast milk is the real key to continued nursing once a mother returns to work. If you are interested in breast-feeding while working, contact your human resources director about where and how you can store your milk. Some companies have pumping stations and offer small refrigerators to mothers in response to the needs of their breast-feeding staff. Think about it this way: Your company wants to keep you because of your valuable skills. Most would rather accommodate a worker and keep her working than lose her because of a lack of effort on their part.

BENEFITS OF BREAST-FEEDING TO MOTHERS
Breast-feeding isn't just a good choice in terms of a baby's health. It offers benefits to mothers as well.

Mothers who breast-feed get an extra pumping of oxytocin in their bloodstream when their babies suckle or even cry that contracts the uterus back to its prepregnant size. There is also evidence that mothers who breast-feed for a period of three months cut their risk of developing breast cancer in half.

More is learned every year about the advantages of breast-feeding and how mothers benefit from it.

It can be hard to survive working and breast-feeding without continued support from a partner. But a partner is just part of the circle. You matter most of all. Turning what have essentially been sexual objects back into basic, utilitarian items takes some getting used to. It helps that throughout pregnancy, your breasts have altered, becoming fuller, more sensitive, and prepared for breast-feeding without your having to do a thing; your body does it for you, growing and swelling in preparation for your baby's first feeding.

SEEKING PROFESSIONAL HELP
Sometimes the guidance and support of a partner, a doula, or a friend is not enough. During highly stressful or potentially complicated breast-feeding situations, a mother is best served by professional breast-feeding information and solutions. It is

during these times that a mother should seek out La Leche League leaders (who are trained in support) and lactation consultants. As opposed to the informal nature of La Leche League meetings, lactation consultants often work in a hospital or for a doctor or midwife, offering clinic or home consultation and advice for breast-feeding moms. These professionals have gone through extensive training and can be life savers for mothers who are receiving conflicting advice from other health professionals.

You can find an international board certified lactation consultant in your area on the World Wide Web at www.iblce.org. La Leche League International's site has breast-feeding information, books, and other resources. Its Web site can be accessed at www.lalecheleague.org.

Most of the discomfort and swelling will disappear within the first week. You can apply cold compresses or warm washcloths to alleviate any tightness within the milk glands. It is possible for breasts to become engorged with breast milk before the supply-and-demand system between the baby and the milk glands gets under way. Do not get stressed about this. Simply nurse your baby and apply compresses if needed. You can also release a tiny bit of milk in the shower, but be careful. Pumping your breasts will only convince your milk glands to make more milk, making the engorged feeling worse!

Of course, none of this may happen if you decide not to nurse your baby. Although I wholeheartedly believe that every baby deserves the beautiful, delicious food her mother makes for her, I also acknowledge that this is a decision, a choice that each mom has to make for herself. As a doula, I support whatever feeding choice a mother makes. Hopefully, whatever choice she makes will be based on as much information as possible.

If you choose to bottle-feed your baby infant formula, you need to be vigilant. Clean all the bottles and nipples with hot, soapy water, sterilize the equipment before use, and throw out any leftover formula. You have to do these things in an effort to keep your baby healthy. Look around your house and consider how you will accomplish the above-mentioned tasks. Some mothers keep a rolling cycle of formulas in the refrigerator that are dated and ready. For a time, keep a schedule and follow it. Your baby's health depends on your taking the necessary steps to ensure her safety from bacteria and germs.

Your physical body has changed irrevocably from the woman you were before pregnancy. Parts of you may look the same, and other parts may have altered considerably. What has also changed, but is less apparent than your physical transformations, is your spirit. Becoming a mother refashions the innermost parts of you into a new person, a woman who cares for and sustains new life.

With this change comes a heightened sense of connection, both with other mothers and with your newborn.

The next chapter discusses your spiritual connection and more.

9

❊ ❊ ❊

YOUR SPIRITUAL
CONNECTION

Mothers today hear story after story of ways people spiritually connect with newborns. From more technical psychological jargon to the popularized notion of bonding, mothers learn about connecting from a variety of sources. In most versions of postbirth connecting, a mother has her baby and then gazes at him in absolute divine splendor, overcome with warm fuzzy feelings that transmit immediate love toward her newborn. This fairy tale did not originate from the careful and loaded bonding studies performed by the Bowlbys and Klauses and Kennells of the world, but from the eagerness of mothers and a health care system to create concrete steps that lead to baby love.

This notion of spiritually connecting, or bonding, may have unfairly pressured mothers to exhibit certain assumed feelings toward their newborns, but it also heralded a more family-centered approach to birth. It is primarily due to the seminal work of pediatricians Marshall Klaus and John Kennell in the early

1970s that women now have the option of "rooming in" with their newborns after birth.

Eager people looking for a list of things that would guarantee happiness, and unconditional newborn love, latched onto the observed maternal and infant behaviors in Klaus and Kennell's research and turned that into a list of must-haves. When birth did not register the requisite emotive responses in mothers, something was presumed wrong with her. The concept of bonding, and all of the assumptions that go with it, has produced an amazing polarity between mothers (and health professionals) who are convinced of its merits, and mothers (and health professionals) who feel that it is an illusion. I have talked with many mothers who experienced guilt because they believed they should have been happy, maternal, and loving toward everyone, including their babies, within minutes of giving birth.

The truth about a mother's connection to her newborn and her postpartum feelings is far more complicated than that. New mothers may grieve their pregnant form, be apprehensive about assuming the responsibility of a defenseless newborn, wonder why their minds haven't immediately accepted that the babies in their wombs became the babies in their arms, and even worry whether they are capable of doing a "good" job of mothering. All of these things and maybe, just maybe, an overwhelming feeling of love are part of the spiritual and emotional connection experienced by a new mother.

Although most of the interest in maternal and infant connections has focused on bonding, a number of researchers have focused on the biological and neurochemical cues a mother engages in with her newborn, even without her knowledge, that strengthens their relationship. Far from being a passive recipient of caretaking, babies are just as involved in their own dynamic spiritual and biological interactions with their mothers and other kin. Much can be learned by examining how and why this happens.

SENSORY PERCEPTION

The optimal coordination between the new mammalian mother and her young involves a sequence of behaviors on the part of each that ensures that the young will be adequately cared for and show healthy physical, emotional, and social development. This coordination is accomplished by each member of the relationship having the appropriate sensitivities and responses to cues that characterize the other.

—Fleming et al., "Neurobiology of Mother-Infant
Interactions: Experience and Central Nervous System
Plasticity Across Development and Generations,"
Neuroscience Behavior Review, *1999*

Within moments of giving birth, a new mother and her baby engage in an ages-old dance of awareness and feedback that strives to ensure not love but infant survival. Newborns are fragile creatures who are utterly incapable of caring for themselves. They cannot walk, speak (in terms of forming words), gather food for themselves, or protect themselves. All of these needs are met by a mother, father, and in some cases other kin. They are the ones who will carry, nurture, teach, feed, and clothe the baby.

A newborn baby essentially targets this group of caregivers and starts the long process of attachment that will enable the group, notably the mother, to keep him alive. The subtle cues and feedback mechanisms get more intricate throughout the postpartum period so that by three months, when a mother says something and her baby responds by smiling (something that will delight the mother), the process of attachment is well on its way.

Decades ago, researchers assumed babies did nothing more in the womb and in the newborn stage than be dependent blobs that cried themselves to sleep, demanded food, and needed an endless supply of clean diapers. It was assumed that a parent, or even a stranger, could provide these services. Although adoptive and foster parents can and do attach to newborns who are not biologically theirs, the biological responses that a newborn gives her mother and other family members is strong and well documented.

Newborn babies, having been immersed in the inner world of the womb, come out with a high level of sensory perception. Researchers currently are trying to study the levels of awareness of the unborn baby and the role these sensations play in the postpartum period.

A 1994 study by Fifer and Moon showed that newborns can distinguish between voices postpartum, singling out their mother's voice, and they have a physical response to it. Both in and out of the womb, babies' heart rates decelerate when presented with sounds, something that usually occurs during sleep. The researchers of this study speculate that voices and sounds provide newborns with sensory stimuli that aid in brain development.

Auditory development isn't the only sense that a newborn has cultivated in the womb. While inside his mother, surrounded by amniotic fluid, he swallows this substance, learning what many perceive to be feeding skills that will be useful after birth. As described in the June 2001 issue of *Pediatrics*, researchers Mennella, Jagnow, and Beauchamp introduced a flavor into the diet of pregnant mothers and continued to give it to them once they commenced nursing their newborns. The last part of the experiment was to observe the response of the now solid-food-eating infants to the same flavor introduced in cereal. This intriguing research showed that babies may be conditioned to flavors in a mother's diet by the flavor associations identified in her amniotic fluid and breast milk, enabling the introduction of this flavor directly to the solid-food eating infant to be less stressful, and actually accepting. Previous research already established that flavors enter the amniotic fluid. The *Pe-*

diatrics study is only one of many that is attempting to establish a learning mechanism involved in the sensory perception of amniotic fluid.

But this cushion for the baby in the uterus does even more. A 1996 study by Varendi and others found that babies are attracted to the scents of their own amniotic fluid. Newborn babies located and suckled their mother's amniotic-fluid-swabbed nipple and areola more than they chose a washed nipple. The authors speculate that the smell of amniotic fluid may be familiar to the infant, which may suggest avoiding chemically enhanced baby products that may mask the odor connection between a mother and her baby.

A review article in *Genetica* by Porter discussed the hypothesis that odor may be used by the newborn to recognize kin other than the mother, given the similarities in the metabolism of relatives. This kin recognition may be one of the greatest reasons to involve the family unit after birth in the caring of a newborn. If the baby is able to identify the important people in his or her life by scent, then those individuals should be near the baby to imprint their smell on their new relative.

Newborns, though, are doing much more than just smelling; they are watching and being watched. Studies show that humans prefer the faces of newborn animals, with their circular shape, big eyes, and fat cheeks. Newborn seals, puppies, and human infants elicit "ahs" and "ohs" from adults who find them immensely watchable. This visual cue makes mothers and fathers want to look at and therefore care for their babies. For their part, newborns are able to discern images (without color), especially faces, that are six to twelve inches away from them. Incidentally, this is the exact distance from a mother's breast to her baby's face. As the postpartum phase moves on, a baby expands her viewing ability until she is able to see across the room and then in color.

Although visual acuity takes time, a newborn responds to physical closeness and heat immediately after birth. A nearly guaranteed way to calm fussy newborns is to wear them against your skin in a soft carrier. The beating of your heart (a sound she has grown accustomed to in the womb), the heat of your skin (she was in a 98.6 degree "oven"), and your familiar maternal odor make baby wearing a sensory gold mine in terms of associating with a newborn.

This skin-on-skin contact has become so critical to newborn development that it is used to help regulate and nurture premature babies. Known as kangaroo care, this skin-to-skin holding has been found to stabilize heart and respiratory functions in a newborn and was recently shown, as described in the *American Journal of Maternal Child Nursing,* to possibly play a positive role in lowering the risk for postpartum depression by stabilizing maternal hormone release.

The multifunctionality of touch may also explain the reason that another sense, sound, registers on so many levels. Studies clearly show that a newborn's cry cues a parent to do something to alleviate his discomfort, triggers breast milk letdown in mothers, and raises the stress level of parents. One study showed that although adults may find a newborn's cry uncomfortable to hear, parents have a chemical response to the sound, perhaps a biochemical trigger to care for the distressed infant; again, nature aiding infant survival.

Mothers, just like you, are also giving off sensorial perception cues and feedback signals to their infants, even without their active knowledge. The distress that many new mothers experience worrying about their ability to care for their infants is unnecessary, since the biological signals they emit are so strong. Unfortunately, the added stress and worry about parenting and adjusting to life with a newborn results in hormones being released that may disrupt the hard-wired chemical circuitry between a newborn and a mother. Other chemical signals can disrupt this natural perception, such as analgesia and anesthesia used during labor and birth, drugs for pain and loss of sensation that have the potential to make both baby and mother neurochemically numb and unresponsive to each other.

The goal for every new mother then is not to do a certain list of things to ensure attachment to her newborn, but to listen to her urges and desires in terms caring for her baby. So much that goes on postpartum is subtle but nonetheless is happening.

For example, regardless of whether a mother perceives of these abilities, she can identify her baby:

By smell. Studies consistently show that mothers can recognize their babies among other newborns by scent alone. They also have the ability to pinpoint their baby's amniotic fluid on clothing. One 1998 study showed that fathers can also accurately identify their baby's amniotic fluid.

By touch. Even when given only the back of a hand to stroke, mothers can discern which baby's skin is theirs. Skin, the body's largest organ, is full of nerve and sense endings that actively engage with the other senses of the body. It is not surprising, given how much time a baby spends in her mother's arms, that a mother can recognize her baby by touch alone.

By cry. One study showed that by the second or third day postpartum, more mothers woke up when their own babies cried, versus responding to the cry of other babies nearby. Essentially, mothers learn to recognize the unique sounds of their own babies early in the attachment cycle.

Together, these biochemical sensations, including the many other sensory-rich situations of bathing, nursing, and talking to a newborn, safeguard the spiritual and biological connection between a mother and her baby. This connection, though, does not imply instant feelings of love or maternal contentment. Biological perceptions of the senses happen independently of emotion; however, they are often heightened by emotion.

Mothers like you, anxious to understand their newborns in a deep, intimate way and lessen apprehension and distress, can follow some simple doula hints to facilitate the biological and resulting spiritual connection with their babies.

Some Doula Hints that Encourage the Mother-Infant Connection

Handle your baby. Babies like to be held, touched, and cuddled. This action reinforces tactile, odor, and visual connections between a mother and her baby. Newborns, although they are squirmy, are easy to swaddle and cuddle. As complicated as the swaddling lesson may appear during the first few days postpartum, it really is not as difficult as it appears. The only real rule to follow is always support your newborn's head when she is in your arms. Remember, as smart as newborns are, they are incapable of regulating their muscles or even their body temperature. Soon, though, within months, she will be able to support her own head, encouraging even more cuddling and holding.

Currently, much debate swirls in the parenting world about whether holding a baby encourages her to be spoiled. Regardless of where you fall on the debate, you have to know that biologically, a baby has no ulterior motives beyond surviving. In many ways, the issues about spoiling center on what type of parent an individual mother or father wants to be. Suddenly, perceptions by others become more important than caring for a baby. Please don't make nurturing and caring for your baby become something so theoretical that your baby's needs and desires are ignored.

Look at your baby. We've talked about the beauty of babies, but perhaps that was an overstatement. Newborn babies, especially those born vaginally, often have heads that are molded from being in the birth canal, puffy eyes, blotchy skin color, and genitals enlarged by their mother's pregnancy hormones. Many are covered by white, greasy stuff known as vernix. It helps the baby move through the tight birth canal and offers some infection protection.

Some babies have light hair on their bodies called lanugo. This hair covers their bodies in the womb and falls off after birth, as may the hair on their head.

Newborns look like nothing most parents have ever seen. Yet, even with their cone heads and protruding umbilical cords that have been clamped off close to their stomachs, they appear to most parents as the most beautiful creatures they have ever seen.

At every opportunity, look at your baby. Notice her little fingers. Marvel at her tiny mouth that seems to pucker and stretch at the slightest contact with her cheek. Take in the legs that have been bowed inside the uterus, and guess who she might resemble. When you take off her clothes during a diaper change, really see the body of your baby.

During this entire visual assessment, you are storing facts about your baby. Details like any prominent birthmarks and her primary hair color will become part of your visual coding of your newborn. Each observation adds to the growing list of sensory cues that provide both you and your baby with intricate knowledge of each other.

Smell your baby. There are moments when I am in a crowded place, like a busy coffee shop, that I am literally bowled over by the many scents that dominate the lives of adults. From perfumes to lotions and even soaps, we wear, spray, or apply scents that mask our natural body odor.

The mingling of this potpourri can be unpleasant to inhale for a knowledgeable adult, but it is simply stifling and confusing for a newborn. For your baby's sensitive nose, limit the lotions, shampoos, conditioners, or soaps that you use. If it is possible, change brands and types of certain items to ones that have less perfume. Luckily, today there is a resurgent interest in natural products. Many health food stores and even regular grocery stores carry product lines of organic items.

Limiting odors also applies to the items you place on your baby's skin. A newborn's skin is sensitive. When he is first born, his skin has to adapt to new tactile sensations.

Unfortunately, many of the infant products on the market are full of artificially derived fragrances that are aimed at parents, not babies. These companies reach out to mothers just like you when they prepare these items by putting together scents that smell like many people think a baby should smell. But that supposed fresh scent is not the real odor of a newborn. Every newborn has his own combined smell—intermingled milk, sweat, and that unidentifiable scent that a mother can detect at her baby's temple.

No powder, lotion, or bath soap will ever mimic that. In fact, it may actually hinder a baby's natural scent and a baby's connection with its mother. When foreign odors waft around a new mother and her baby, they may not be aware of each other on a biological level.

Talk to your baby. It is well documented that babies can identify sound while they are in the womb. One interesting review of studies of auditory learning in infants found that babies, in the womb and out, can recognize pitch differences, rhythm, and stress in speech.

Some studies have even shown a preference among babies for high-pitched voices, which may suggest a predisposition for their mother's voice.

In any event, language development and auditory stimulation happen because of communication. The more a baby is talked to, the more stimulation she receives. Although this does not translate to advanced language development, it is part of an infant's general language acquisition.

One 2001 study showed that babies as young as two weeks old emit a "mama" utterance that parents interpret as a wanting or an attention-getting sound. This language development continues throughout a young baby's life, allowing him to overhear words and eventually mimic and then test certain sounds.

Speaking to a newborn, a being that one researcher says has a natural innate sense of language, would show any mother how much her baby loves her voice. Whether it is the close proximity of the speaker that entreats them, or the familiarity of the voice, newborns love hearing their parents.

When you start talking to your baby, try not to concentrate on what you say. Let the words flow freely. If you would like to talk about your goals as a parent, fine. Many mothers talk to their babies in a personal way until their newborns appear to understand their words. This recognition, though, is happening as early as the first few weeks after birth. One study described in *Developmental Neuropsychology* found that although newborns could not distinguish complex speech stimuli, they could discriminate changes in speech patterns.

Yet speech pattern recognition is only one benefit of talking to your baby. The other component is an increase in mother and baby connection and interaction. A study in the journal *Birth* found that mothers who roomed in with their babies talked to and touched them more, versus interacting with the television or the telephone. This increased interaction may well lead to a less stressful relationship. Why? Contact breeds familiarity.

Breast-feed your baby. There is indisputable evidence that breast-feeding rolls every sensory stimuli together for the benefit of both mother and baby. Babies and mothers interact during nursing, combining touch, smell, taste, visual interaction, and usually nonsensical speech. Essentially, from a biological standpoint, breast-feeding presents the mother lode of connection.

From the initial grasping of the nipple by a newborn to her fast and then slow sucking pattern and settling into a sated sleep, breast-feeding babies interact with their mothers in a continual loop of maternal responsiveness and newborn feedback. Every time your baby is positioned in your arms, pay close attention to the way you feel.

Breast-feeding offers so many benefits to both mother and baby that choosing not to give a baby this food has to be considered carefully. Unfortunately, there are mothers in our society who lack continuous support that would enable them to extend nursing beyond the first few weeks after birth, including the financial freedom to remain with their babies as long as they would like. Even with the complexities of both support and time, the biology and the benefits of breast-feeding remain important.

For those mothers who choose not to nurse their babies, it is imperative that they connect with their babies during feeding. I am always distressed when I see a mother prop a bottle of formula for her baby who may be sleeping in a car seat. Never rob your baby of sensory connection with you or another family member. For many weeks, this connection is vital to a baby's development.

When mothers connect with their babies, no matter what else is going on in their lives, they are creating a foundation of spiritual connection on which to build.

In time, this connection often leads to an intense feeling of love and responsibility. As you develop your relationship with your baby, rest assured that biology is working with you, strengthening your spiritual, deeply intimate connection to your baby.

Motherhood, the amazing journey that you have started, is about much more than just questions, concerns, steps, or biology. Motherhood is an act of giving, of raising a precious being into an adult.

It will take all of you, all of the various parts of your whole being, to navigate this journey with strength and courage.

✤ ✤ ✤

FINAL THOUGHTS

Throughout this book, I have shared suggestions and offered advice for living and for being a healthy, holistically centered mother. Many of these ideas benefit any woman who seeks to navigate life as a whole person.

Throughout your motherhood journey, I hope that you continue to build the layers of yourself and grow as a mother. Be prepared, though, for this experience to extend beyond your baby's infancy and into the years beyond. Motherhood doesn't end just because health professionals stop talking about it after the months of postpartum. This process for you has only just begun.

From my heart, I wish you and your new family nothing but happiness, peace, and love.

A QUICK TAKE ON DOULAS

Doulas are women who offer continuous emotional, mental, and physical support to mothers during pregnancy, childbirth, and the first weeks or months postpartum. Although doulas are relatively new members of the childbirth team, their service of mothering and comforting mothers dates back generations to a time when women from a mother's community aided her while she guided her baby into the world.

Today a doula is a professional trained in birth physiology and the dynamics of childbearing. The women who become doulas are often health professionals who want to provide additional services and skills to families.

If you are interested in finding a doula for your baby's birth, or one who can assist you during the early weeks of recovery postpartum, contact Doulas of North America or the Association of Labor Assistants and Childbirth Educators. You can find their contact information in the resource section at the end of the book.

RESOURCES FOR HELP,
ADVICE, AND INSPIRATION

This list includes only a small sampling of the numerous resources available to childbearing women. Each source is trusted and respected for accurate, up-to-date information.

Mothering
(magazine)
P.O. Box 1690
Santa Fe, NM 87504
www.mothering.com

Cascade Healthcare Products, Inc.
(a mail-order birth supply and bookstore, Birth and Life)
141 Commercial NE
P.O. Box 12203
Salem, OR 97301
www.1cascade.com

American College of Nurse Midwives
818 Connecticut Ave., NW, Suite 900
Washington, D.C. 20006
www.midwife.org

Association of Labor Assistants and Childbirth Educators
(an organization that trains and certifies childbirth
educators and labor assistants or birth doulas)
P.O. Box 390436
Cambridge, MA 02139
www.alace.org

Coalition for Improving Maternity Services
(a coalition of individuals and organizations committed
to improving maternity care)
P.O. Box 2346
Ponte Vedra Beach, FL 32004
www.motherfriendly.org

Doulas of North America
(an organization that trains and certifies
birth and postpartum doulas)
P.O. Box 626
Jasper, IN 47547
www.dona.org

**Global Maternal/Child Health Association and
Waterbirth International**
(an organization that promotes and supports
mothers, families, and waterbirth)
P.O. Box 366
West Linn, OR 97068
www.waterbirth.org

International Childbirth Education Association
(an organization that certifies and trains childbirth
educators, doulas, and other birth professionals)
P.O. Box 20048
Minneapolis, MN 55240–0048
www.icea.org

La Leche League
(the premier breast-feeding advocacy and
support organization)
9616 Minneapolis Avenue
Franklin Park, IL 60131
www.lalecheleague.org

Lamaze International
2025 M Street, Suite 800
Washington, D.C. 20036–3309
www.lamaze-childbirth.com

Midwives Alliance of North America
P.O. Box 175
Newton, KS 67114
www.mana.org

March of Dimes Birth Defects Foundation
1275 Mamaroneck Avenue
White Plains, NY 10605
www.modimes.org

National Association of Childbearing Centers
3123 Gottschall Road
Perkiomenville, PA 18074
www.birthcenters.org

INDEX